Muriel Rukeyser's

The Book of the Dead

Muriel Rukeyser's

The Book of the Dead

Tim Dayton

University of Missouri Press
Columbia

Copyright © 2003 by
The Curators of the University of Missouri
First paperback printing, 2015
University of Missouri Press, Columbia, Missouri 65201
Printed and bound in the United States of America
All rights reserved
5 4 3 2 1   19 18 17 16 15

Cataloging-in-Publication data available from the Library of Congress

ISBN 978-0-8262-2063-9

♾™ This paper meets the requirements of the
American National Standard for Permanence of Paper
for Printed Library Materials, Z39.48, 1984.

Designer: Jennifer Cropp
Typesetter: Bookcomp, Inc.
Typefaces: Palatino, Vendome, Bodoni

For my mother and father

Contents

Acknowledgments

I have had the help of countless people in the years since I began working on *The Book of the Dead;* none of them are responsible for this book's shortcomings, nor for the positions I take up. The staff of the Interlibrary Services department of Hale Library, Kansas State University, was consistently cheerful and efficient in tracking down obscure material. The special-collections librarians of the University of Delaware; Brown University; Syracuse University; the Library of Congress; and the Berg Collection, New York Public Library, provided me with invaluable assistance. In particular, Stephen Crook of the Berg Collection provided help in the early stages of the project, when I was still feeling my way. Beverly Jarrett, Jane Lago, and Gary Kass of the University of Missouri Press oversaw the transformation of my manuscript into a book with great professionalism and care. Finally, by way of institutional acknowledgments, Kansas State University provided me with a much-needed sabbatical midway through the project, as well as a research grant that made it possible for me to meet Muriel Rukeyser's son and literary executor, William, and to study those papers of hers that he has kept in his possession.

Several classes of undergraduate and graduate students at Kansas State University have been subjected both to my general obsessions—to which all my students are liable—and to my obsessions specific to *The Book of the Dead,* and I thank them for indulging me. In particular I found the comments and questions of Sarah Caldwell, Jim Hohenbary, and Kirsten Young of use as I was developing my thoughts about Rukeyser's poem. A former student, David Kruger, served ably as a research assistant, saving me a good deal of time and money that would have been spent on travel. Mary Siegle, secretary of the Department of English, cheerfully provided *very* timely assistance with typing.

I was given information that proved helpful in the construction of my argument by William Rukeyser and Alan Wald, both of whom were uncommonly generous. I am indebted also to a number of individuals who read all or part of this book in manuscript form. Donna Potts and Larry Rodgers read an early essay version and provided valuable comments that showed me some possible lines of development I could follow once I decided that my project was book-length in scope. The anonymous readers for the *Journal of Modern Literature,* as well as editor-in-chief Morton Levitt, provided valuable suggestions and criticisms that improved the essay I eventually published in that journal. I use portions of that essay, "Lyric and Document in Muriel Rukeyser's *The Book of the Dead"* (*Journal of Modern Literature* 21:2 [Winter 1997]: 223–40), in this book. Jamie Owen Daniel and Jerry Dees read the first manuscript version of this book and gave me countless valuable suggestions at a point when I was incapable of seeing my own work clearly anymore. My anonymous readers at the University of Missouri Press also helped me to improve the manuscript considerably, and I am grateful for their efforts.

Finally, I would like to thank members of my family. My mother and father, Shirley and William Dayton, provided various kinds of support through the years that made it possible for me to get to the point where I could actually do something like write a book. My uncle, Cliff Dayton, was an intelligent, well-read man without the benefit of higher education; he helped provide the impetus for this book through his example and through his insistence when I was young that I get as much education as I could stand. My wife, Angela Hubler, patiently read virtually every version of this work with a fine combination of rigor and generosity. She was always there when I needed her, which was often. Our two children, Neil and Jack, provided no such help (although they did occasionally ask how I was doing, once they got old enough) and no doubt added years to the time it took to finish the thing. They, however, provided their own form of help: those all-important games of marbles, Lego-building sessions, and late-afternoon soccer practices that kept what I was doing in perspective, in more ways than one.

Muriel Rukeyser's

The Book of the Dead

Introduction

Following many years of relative neglect and obscurity, Muriel Rukeyser's *The Book of the Dead* has recently been returned to print and become the subject of critical attention.[1] This book continues that trend, though I began work on it before the recent spate of interest began to manifest itself. I taught *The Book of the Dead* to a mixed undergraduate and graduate student class on "American Literature, 1910–1950" at Kansas State University in the fall semester, 1993. I had become aware of the poem because of a talk by Cary Nelson at the 1989 convention of the Modern Language Association, and had determined to teach it the first chance that I got. At that time there was very little published on the poem, so I was forced to do nearly all the primary critical work myself. I had no sooner made a beginning on this than I realized that there was an enormous amount and variety of such work to be done, and to that work I have devoted much of my research time over the past nine years.

After these years of working on *The Book of the Dead* I have concluded that it stakes out a distinctive and important position in modern poetry, and more specifically within the leftist tradition in modern poetry. The most efficient way I can think to make this distinctive quality clear is by relating it to two different, and in many ways opposing, traditions in leftist letters, that of Bertolt Brecht and that of Theodor Adorno. By understanding—however schematically—*The Book of the Dead* within these traditions, one may see that the poem's political significance and its aesthetic and formal significance, while not identical, are at least closely related and mutually reinforcing.

The Book of the Dead may be related to the poetic project of Brecht—and I refer specifically to the *poetic* project, as opposed to the not-unrelated

1. The poem appears in Cary Nelson, ed., *Anthology of Modern American Poetry* (New York: Oxford University Press, 2000), and in Kate Daniels, ed., *Out of Silence: Selected Poems of Muriel Rukeyser* (1992; reprint, Evanston, Ill.: Northwestern University Press, 1995).

dramatic project—insofar as it attempts to break with the self-enclosed quality of the modern lyrical subject. Brecht rejected the tradition of the lyric as it presented itself to him because it was unacceptably subjectivist in form, caught up within the dimensions of a somewhat fantastically iso- lated subjectivity.[2] He attempted in his poetry to achieve something dif- ferent from this, to create a speaking subject whose being derived from "the outside" as much as from "the inside"; or rather, a speaking subject in whom the interrelation of inside and outside would be dynamic and meaningful. By allowing the outside world, the world of historical experi- ence, to have a meaningful place within lyrical speech, Brecht attempted to produce a poetry free from what he saw as the ideological character—and self-indulgence—of the modern lyric, which rendered it essentially con- servative in character. Readers familiar with Brecht's poetry will, I hope, agree with this description, whether or not they share my opinion that on the whole Brecht came remarkably near achieving what he aimed for.

What Brecht distrusted, Adorno redeemed; the isolated lyric speaker emerges from Adorno's "Lyric Poetry and Society" as a nearly heroic fig- ure, both preserving social experience in the only form in which it is *experi- ence*—all social experience being necessarily individual in character—and holding out against those forces operative in capitalist society that threaten to destroy the "bourgeois" subjectivity that is one of the great, if contra- dictory, historical achievements of the capitalist era. Adorno's essay thus identifies the necessarily social nature of all lyrical utterance—a necessity established by the ontological priority of the social to the individual and seen most concretely in the social nature of the very material of poetry, language—and by this means clarifies the value of the lyrical subject as such. While Adorno's position does not directly oppose that of Brecht, it does contrast with it, since Adorno was at least as concerned with pre- serving the subjective element in lyric speech as he was with revealing the implicit links between this subjective element and the world of social experience.

Muriel Rukeyser seems to have understood, largely in a creative, "intu- itive," rather than fully analytical way, the emphases of both Brecht and Adorno and to have determined to find a form in which the problems to which they point might be overcome. (Obviously, I am not arguing for "in- fluence" here: while Rukeyser would have been aware of Brecht at the time she wrote *The Book of the Dead* in the 1930s, Adorno's "Lyric Poetry and So- ciety" was not published until 1957.) While Rukeyser was as attuned to the general intellectual and artistic problems of the day as anyone, she no doubt felt the problem of the lyric speaker with particular, personal force. *Theory of Flight* (1935), her first volume, had been widely praised, but there

2. Philip Thomson, *The Poetry of Brecht: Seven Studies*, 1–12.

were widespread objections to the vagueness or diffuseness of her lyric po-
ems. They seemed, to many readers, overly subjective, and Rukeyser felt
she needed to confront the objective world more fully in her work.

Rukeyser's attempted solution both to her specific problem and to the
more general problem confronting leftist poets of reconciling "lyric and so-
ciety" is found in the form of *The Book of the Dead*, with its combination, in
my analysis at least, of the three classical modes of lyric, epic, and dramatic.
Thus the formal strategies of the poem are directly linked to some of its cen-
tral political concerns, and my formal analysis is never wholly unrelated to
politics. Indeed, to fully understand the magnitude of the poem one must
appreciate the interaction of the formal and political problems Rukeyser
faced when she undertook to write *The Book of the Dead*. That said, for some
readers, I fear, there will be too much politics, for others too little, while I,
of course, hope to have gotten it just right.

This is probably the best point at which to introduce alongside Brecht and
Adorno yet a third figure from the pantheon of twentieth-century Marxism,
Ernst Bloch, whose pioneering work in utopian hermeneutics provides one
of the constant, though not always explicit, reference points of this book.
While this is not the place for a protracted discussion of Bloch, it should be
noted that the central understanding I have formed of *The Book of the Dead*
is deeply informed by Bloch, and particularly by his dynamic conception of
the utopian function. For Bloch, utopia is not so much the carefully delin-
eated, rationally blueprinted projection of the ideal world, or an impossibly
perfect never-never land, but rather a figure of the real possibility of human
emancipation from the oppressive structures imposed by class society and
a critical principle springing from the real inadequacies of the present.

The utopian function of art and literature, then, is that of a critical edge
undercutting resignation—whether happy or unhappy—to the present. To
understand the world through the register of the utopian is to read the
signs of movement—or rather the *potential* for movement—toward "the
overthrow (instead of the hypocritical new installation) of all conditions in
which the human individual is a humiliated, enslaved, forsaken, despised
creature."[3] It is also to read in the things of the world, including works
of art and literature, figures—however partial—of reconciliation between
humans and nature and between human and human. For Bloch's Marxist
practice of utopian interpretation, utopian possibility is rooted in the real
non-utopia of the present rather than in some cloud-cuckoo-land, a desir-
able state unrelated and without any pathway to reality.

It is only by means of an interpretive practice such as that elaborated by
Bloch—one that, whether Rukeyser read Bloch or not, bears considerable
resemblance to the artistic method and intellectual outlook she developed

3. Jack Zipes, "Toward a Realization of Anticipatory Illumination," xxv.

from the resources available to her—that one can see *The Book of the Dead* as a utopian text. Or rather, it is only by means of a way of reading that is able to perceive the interrelation of horror and hope in *The Book of the Dead* that its utopian contents become visible. The title of the poem, of course, might by itself indicate that it is not in any immediate way utopian, and its central topic, the death by silicosis of hundreds of tunnel workers, is about as remote from the utopian as one can imagine. But, as I have attempted to make plain in what follows, the poem is rich in what Raymond Williams refers to as "resources for a journey of hope."[4] It is in her insistence on this radical hope, as well as in her more obvious willingness to root her poem in the topical ground of a horrifying, preventable industrial disaster, that Rukeyser produced a profoundly moving poem, a searching poem that resonates into both the past and the future.

4. Raymond Williams, *Towards 2000*, 268.

1

Muriel Rukeyser and the Gauley Tunnel Tragedy

Muriel Rukeyser, living in New York City at the time, kept a weekly record for 1937, of which the page for September 23–28 is apparently all that survives. Two lines read:

Sept. 24 . . . Fred Dupee dinner, Nin, Leon, Barcelona.
　　25 . . . Dr. Hess, movies w/ Frances, Sam Sillen. "Blues"[1]

One page is not much, but even these two lines tell us something. Fred, or F. W., Dupee was a founding editor of *Partisan Review* following its revival in 1937. Before that Dupee was briefly the literary editor of the Communist party–sponsored journal *New Masses*. Dupee had left *New Masses*, repulsed by what he saw as the subordination of literary and intellectual integrity to the immediate political concerns of the Communist party.[2] In turning to *Partisan Review*, Dupee aligned himself with a leftist alternative to *New Masses*, whose political and cultural Popular Front ethos emphasized a broadly antifascist as opposed to a specifically socialist politics.

The difference between the political stance of *New Masses* and that of *Partisan Review* paralleled—if only roughly—the difference between the two journals with regard to cultural issues. Originally established in 1934 as the publishing wing of the Communist party's John Reed Clubs, *Partisan*

1. Muriel Rukeyser Papers, Library of Congress. The quasi-biographical material in this chapter is intended to serve as a way into *The Book of the Dead*. There is not as yet a full biography of Rukeyser available. Of the biographical sketches published, I find that in Alan Wald's *Exiles from a Future Time: The Forging of the Mid-Twentieth-Century Literary Left* (299–306) to be the most informative, particularly for those aspects of Rukeyser's career that are directly relevant to *The Book of the Dead*.

2. Terry Cooney, *The Rise of the New York Intellectuals:* Partisan Review *and Its Circle*, 100–102; Alan Wald, *The New York Intellectuals*, 86–87.

Review first merged with another politically radical literary journal, *Anvil*, then folded altogether in 1936. Reestablished in 1937 as an independent journal, the revived *Partisan Review* attempted to combine modernist aesthetics and anti-Stalinist, quasi-Trotskyist leftist politics into a progressive cultural force that both respected the integrity of cultural production and adhered to political principle. Dupee solicited a poem from Rukeyser for the revived journal (over dinner on the 24th of September?), and Rukeyser responded, although the poem never appeared in *Partisan Review*.[3]

What appears to be the first topic of conversation listed by Rukeyser, "Nin," gives a sense not only of her concerns in September 1937, but also of the political complexity of her world. Andres Nin was the leader of the Partido Obrera de Unificacion Marxista, or POUM. The POUM was a non-Communist party of the Left, strong in Catalonia and a significant force in the Spanish civil war, with its own militia fighting against Franco's Nationalists. In short, "The POUM were a serious group of revolutionary Spanish Marxists, well-led, and independent of Moscow."[4] This strength would prove to be the party's, and Nin's, undoing as it made them an object of the Stalinist campaign to subordinate or destroy the autonomous parties of the Spanish Left.

The most dramatic event in the Stalinist campaign against the POUM was a period of open fighting between the POUM and the Partido Unita Socialista de Catalonia, or PUSC—the Catalonian branch of the Partido Communista de Espana—in Barcelona in May 1937. To be brief, the Soviets feared that the POUM and others of the non-Communist Left would undermine the coalition Republican government because of the radicalism of their programs. This could weaken the ability of the Republicans to prosecute the war against the Nationalists, and hence contribute to the strength of fascism and act to the detriment of the USSR. The Spanish revolution, in short, was subordinated to the priority of the Stalinist program of building "socialism in one country," the USSR. In addition, the POUM and other leftist groups independent of the Stalinist-dominated Communists threatened to weaken the Communist party hegemony of leftist politics. As part of the campaign against the POUM, Nin was arrested on June 16, 1937, along with the other members of the POUM executive committee, and accused of seeking to subvert the Republican government "through violence and the installation of a dictatorship of the proletariat."[5] Ironically—if correctly—the Communists accused Nin and the POUM of being revolutionaries.

Nin was an internationally known figure, and when he disappeared under arrest a good deal of concern was expressed about his fate. But by August 8, 1937, the *New York Times* reported: "Although every effort has been

3. Cooney, *Rise of the New York Intellectuals*, 111, 297 n. 48.
4. Hugh Thomas, *The Spanish Civil War*, 523.
5. Pierre Broué and Emile Témime, *The Revolution and the Civil War in Spain*, 300.

made to hush up the affair, it is now a matter of common knowledge that he was found dead on the outskirts of Madrid, a victim of assassins." The *Times,* while hardly sympathetic to Nin or the POUM, published several pieces on the Nin affair in August 1937. Also in August, Trotsky published a letter (in Russian) about Nin that, while wrong about some factual matters obscured by the secrecy surrounding Nin's abduction and murder, correctly identified the agents of Stalin as culpable.[6]

By contrast, the New York Communist publication the *Daily Worker,* in a number of front-page stories, presented the POUM's conflict with the PUSC as an instance of Trotskyist subversion of the Republican government, which in turn was presented as part of the Trotskyist alliance with fascism. A February 8, 1937, headline read "SPAIN BANS 'POUM' AS ALLY OF FRANCO: Police Ordered to Break Up Trotskyite Group in All Loyalist Spain as Plot against Popular Front is Exposed." When open fighting broke out in May, it was characterized as follows: "FRANCO'S SPIES AND TROT-SKYITES PLOTTED STRIFE IN BARCELONA" (May 8, 1937). When the leaders of the POUM were arrested in June, the *Daily Worker* offered: "TROTZKY-IST PLOT NIPPED IN MADRID: Uprising Planned with Fascists and P.O.U.M." (June 21, 1937). As of September 11, 1937, about two weeks before Rukeyser met with Dupee, the *Daily Worker* continued to maintain that Nin was still alive, having been freed from prison by "a group of Spanish and German armed fascists, agents of the Gestapo." Rukeyser and Dupee would surely be aware that there was good reason to suspect that Nin had been murdered and that the Communist party was behind it.

The next topic of conversation, "Leon," might refer to the Spanish city or province of León; an unknown acquaintance of Rukeyser and Dupee named Leon; or Leon Trotsky, the Bolshevik leader who organized the Red Army and whose role in the Russian Revolution was second in importance only to that of Lenin. The province and the city of León, located in northwestern Spain, were involved in the first months of the war, but were effectively inactive sectors by September 1937 and had been so for about six months. Thus it appears unlikely that it would rank with "Barcelona" as a topic. As to an unknown Leon, that of course must exist as a possibility, yet given Rukeyser and Dupee's other topics of conversation and the events surrounding that conversation, it seems more than likely that "Leon" refers to Trotsky: when Rukeyser and Dupee had dinner on September 24, the Moscow Trials were under way. The trials saw Trotsky and countless others—numerous "old Bolsheviks" prominent among them—accused by Stalin of crimes against the revolution. An investigation into the charges made against Trotsky was led by the eminent American philosopher John

6. Ibid., 267–68.

Dewey, culminating in the public announcement on September 21 that Trotsky was not guilty.

Trotsky was thus very much in the news in late September 1937, but Dupee's level of interest in him would likely have surpassed that of the press. In April 1937 he had written to fellow *Partisan Review* editor Dwight Macdonald: "I don't know anything about Trotzky. I must read him!" In an interview with Alan Wald in 1973, Dupee said: "There's no question that Leon Trotsky definitely influenced me more than any American did. Many radical-liberal intellectuals in the 1930s worshiped FDR, but I never did."[7] Apparently Dupee's admiration for Trotsky came from more than a casual reading, since he went on to edit and introduce a single-volume edition of Max Eastman's translation of Trotsky's three-volume *History of the Russian Revolution*. Quite likely Dupee did his initial reading of Trotsky during the spring and summer of 1937, as he and the other editors of *Partisan Review* were arming themselves intellectually for open warfare with the intellectuals associated with the Communist party. It is hardly surprising, then, that Dupee and Rukeyser talked about "Leon."

"Barcelona" refers to the Spanish civil war, the outbreak of which Rukeyser witnessed, first in the small city of Moncada, and then in the capital of the Catalonia region of Spain, Barcelona. The war pitted the broadly leftist and progressive supporters of the elected government of Spain (the Loyalists or Republicans) against the monarchist, ultraconservatively Catholic, and in some cases avowedly fascistic rightist rebels (the Nationalists). The war was commonly seen as the opening of the conflict between fascist and antifascist forces, as the Nationalists were supported by Mussolini's Italy and Hitler's Germany, while the Loyalists were supported by the Soviet Union and Mexico. Possibly the single most compelling issue of the day for leftists like Rukeyser and Dupee, the Spanish civil war offered—in a complex way—the prospect of one of two futures for Spain, Europe, and the rest of the world as well: fascism or social revolution. Rosa Luxemburg's famous historical alternatives, "socialism or barbarism," appeared to be vying with each other in Spain.

Rukeyser's conversation with Dupee must have been uncomfortable, because for her Barcelona was a city, an event, and a principle with which the internal fighting of the forces on the Left was in conflict. Rukeyser had traveled to Spain in the summer of 1936 as a correspondent for the literary magazine *Life and Letters Today* to cover the People's Olympics, an antifascist alternative to the Olympic games to be held in August in Nazi Germany's capital, Berlin. En route to Spain, Rukeyser spent several weeks in England, mostly in London. Here she visited the editorial offices of *Life and Letters Today* and met, among others, T. S. Eliot, C. Day Lewis, and H.D.

---

7. Wald, *New York Intellectuals*, 163.

(She tried but was unable to meet the Scottish nationalist and Marxist poet Hugh MacDiarmid, who was at the time living on the remote island of Whalsay, in the Shetlands.) She arrived in Spain on July 19, two days after the war started in Spanish Morocco and just as it was spreading to the Spanish mainland. Her train was stopped by fighting in Moncada, a few miles outside Barcelona. Both in Moncada and in Barcelona, to which she traveled in an armed truck on July 21, Rukeyser saw the confusing but inspiring opening of the war.[8]

In her prose accounts of those days in Spain, Rukeyser emphasizes the exhilaration felt by those for whom open conflict with the forces of reaction was preferable to the long period of tension that followed the series of right-wing victories in Hungary, Italy, and elsewhere in Europe, culminating in Hitler's election to the German presidency in 1933. The conflict in Spain offered the possibility, first, of reversing the tide of military and political defeats suffered by the European Left following the initial victory of the Russian Revolution, defeats that resulted in a number of fascist or more traditionally reactionary governments. Second, the conflict seemed to hold the possibility of moving forward, of not only defeating the forces of reaction, but also advancing social revolution. The interconnection of these elements as well as the excitement of the moment manifest themselves toward the end of her account of her experience in Spain for *New Masses*, where she describes a rally of the Loyalist militia and the athletes who had come for the People's Olympics:

> The athletes and the groups with them marched halfway through Barcelona in a tremendous demonstration with the people's army, all wearing strips of black for that week's dead. As the army passed, team after team sang the "Internationale": Norwegian, Dutch, English, Belgian, German, Italian, Hungarian, American. Later, knowing that Italian money and guns were behind the Fascists in Spain . . . , an Italian boy shouted to the people: "The Italian people are with you, watching your victory—and when we get our chance——!" The rest was drowned in a burst of *vivas* and cheering.[9]

The struggle against reaction in Spain, as the account of the Italian boy testifies, was seen to mark the turning of the tide of reaction, and as the arena in which latent revolutionary forces could emerge. While in 1936 Rukeyser

8. Rukeyser published accounts of her trip to Spain in *Life and Letters Today* ("Barcelona, 1936"), *New Masses* ("Death in Spain: Barcelona on the Barricades"), and, nearly forty years later, in *Esquire* ("We Came for Games"). Details about her trip to England are from letters to Horace Gregory and Marya Zaturenska, June 25, 1936, and July 8, 1936, Horace Gregory Papers, Department of Special Collections, Syracuse University Library; and a note in container 1 and a letter from Catherine Carswell, July 17, 1936, Rukeyser Papers.

9. Muriel Rukeyser, "Death in Spain: Barcelona on the Barricades," 11.

presented the opening of the war in terms of a simple conflict between fascism and a popular revolutionary movement of the Left, her conversation in September 1937 with Dupee indicates that she was by that time aware of the moral and political complexities that emerged during the progress of the war.

But the Spanish civil war, "Barcelona," took on deep and unique personal meaning for Rukeyser not only because of its objective significance in the unfolding world conflict, nor just because it was a world-historical event that she happened to have seen in its opening moments, but also because Otto Boch fought in it. Boch was a German athlete, a leftist on his way to the People's Olympics, whom Rukeyser met on the train from Paris to Moncada and with whom she fell swiftly and lastingly in love. When Rukeyser had to leave Spain because she possessed no skills of which the government had need, Boch remained: "He had found his chance to fight fascism, and a profound quiet, amounting to joy, was there."[10] Without ceasing to be a real person for Rukeyser, Boch also became for her a symbol, simultaneously public and private, of hope for a better future wedded to the determination to fight to bring it into being. Killed in battle near Valfonga on April 11, 1938, Boch would figure in Rukeyser's writing throughout her life.

On the 25th of September, Rukeyser apparently had an appointment with a "Dr. Hess," presumably a routine medical visit. She also went to the movies with one "Frances," probably her sister, Frances Rukeyser. Apparently accompanying the sisters—the telegraphic style of the entry makes it difficult to say with certainty—was Samuel Sillen, an editor of *New Masses.* Sillen had begun working at the journal in 1936 and was Fred Dupee's assistant until the day Dupee quit in disgust, saying to Sillen as he left: "You know, I really can't take any more of this."[11] Sillen remained with *New Masses,* eventually becoming literary editor, and stuck with it after its name change to *Masses and Mainstream* and the precipitous general decline of the Communist party in the United States after the Second World War. Some months after their meeting on September 25, 1937, Sillen conducted a radio interview with Rukeyser in which they discussed her recently published volume of poetry, *U.S. 1.* This is the book that contains the long poem *The Book of the Dead*—of which "Blues," or rather, "George Robinson: Blues," the poem she worked on that day, is a part.

So in the course of these two days Rukeyser, in addition to visiting the doctor and taking in a movie, socialized with two people centrally involved, though in dramatically divergent ways, in the literary Left of the

10. Muriel Rukeyser, "We Came for Games," 369.
11. Wald, *New York Intellectuals,* 87.

mid- to late thirties, and conversed with them about the most compelling issues of the day. She was also at work on *The Book of the Dead*, the long poem that would comprise half of her next volume of poetry. These details of Rukeyser's daily existence in 1937 are neither trivia—as would be, say, the fact that she had popcorn when she went to the movies—nor simply the banalities of the life of a writer in that time and place. What could be for some writers the backdrop to their creative life was for Rukeyser to a great extent the *material* of her creative life.

That Rukeyser met with both Dupee and Sillen in the course of two days also provides a glimpse of the broader political context in which she wrote *The Book of the Dead*. While she never joined the Communist party as a member, she did travel in party circles, worked briefly for the *Daily Worker*, and appeared with reasonable frequency in the pages of *New Masses*. In a tellingly ambivalent statement in a letter dated December 20, 1936, Rukeyser wrote to John Wheelwright: "When I was there [Catalonia] I wanted to join the C.P.—came back, and didn't, again." The exact nature of the relationship between Rukeyser and the Communist party, and also the significance for her of Spain (or more precisely, Barcelona), is best characterized by a statement she made in an interview in the *New York Quarterly* in the early 1970s. Talking about her time in Spain, Rukeyser emphasized the "united front" character of the Spain she saw and the sense it gave her of a future that had not yet come to pass:

> The people I was among were the Catalans. These were anarchists—a united front in which anarchists and socialists and communists were within the re- public. . . . It was an extraordinary sight of something that then did not take place. . . . It was a curious vision of a twentieth-century world which would not take place. It may still, but it has been beaten down in place after place, from Spain to Vietnam and many many places in between.[12]

Clearly Rukeyser felt the appeal of the Communist party, yet as her meeting with Dupee and her significant friendship with the Trotskyist Wheelwright

12. Rukeyser to Wheelwright, December 20, 1936, John Wheelwright Collection, John Hay Library, Brown University; Muriel Rukeyser, interview by Cornelia P. Draves and Mary Joyce Fortunato, in *The Craft of Poetry: Interviews from the* New York Quarterly, 172–73. Rukeyser's comments to Alan Wald in an unpublished interview he conducted in New York in May 1976 strike a note similar to that of the *New York Quarterly* interview: "[W]hat I was doing [in the 1930s] was reporting for the *Daily Worker*. I wanted very much for the Communist party as I invented it, as I thought of it, to be something that I could be close to, but I was unable to do that. As I came closer and closer, I went further and further. . . . The closest moment was the moment, and the thing that I wanted most, was the United Front, and I saw that in the first days of the Spanish War, not in Spain proper but in Catalonia, where socialists, anarchists, Communists, trade unions, and gypsies were together in a United Front" (quoted in Alan Wald, letter to the author, October 10, 2001).

shows, she was not one of those for whom the Communist party *was* the Left. Rukeyser was certainly attracted to it (in particular, to its progressive stance on labor and civil rights and its antifascism), but at the same time found it necessary to maintain some distance from it.

If this reading out from and interpretation of the two days in September 1937 recorded in Rukeyser's daybook is accurate, it suggests the fundamental correctness of Michael Denning's approach to the 1930s in his book *The Cultural Front*, in which he attempts to move our vision of that decade beyond the Cold War–era obsession with whether or not certain individuals were members of the Communist party by presenting the era as one in which the party was one important force among others, combining as well as conflicting with various non-Communist leftist groups and individuals.[13] By the very nature of his project, Denning must avoid discussing at any length the quite real and much-discussed sectarian divisions within the leftist movement of the 1930s in order to concentrate on the shared culture that united the Left, despite its divisions, as a counterhegemonic movement. Denning presents this shared culture as more fundamental than the divisions, and this does indeed explain how Rukeyser could have dinner with Fred Dupee one day and go to the movies with Sam Sillen the next, or exchange frequent letters with John Wheelwright and publish in *New Masses*.

While Denning's approach is useful and productive, he errs somewhat in minimizing the conflicts within the Left. The sense one gets of life on the Left from *The Cultural Front* does not really explain how it was that Horace Gregory, at that time the poetry editor for *New Masses*, felt compelled to write to Rukeyser in Spring 1937:

> I suppose you know all about the new backing for the Partisan Review which is Morris money and co-editorship of Dwight Macdonald and Dupee. The chances of its real success are fifty-fifty. The boys have the undying hatred of the League of American Writers & now they've definitely broken Party connections. . . . In NY the whole Stalinist-Trotskyite fight is dangerously provincial: on one side you have the Cowleys who are reviving dead horses in the name of a united front; on the other you have the younger group, under the Partisan Review banner that is allowing itself to adopt the coloring of Trotskyite Marxism. Both movements at the present moment reflect reactionary tendencies. Both movements carry the stigmata of rotten

13. Michael Denning, *The Cultural Front: The Laboring of American Culture in the Twentieth Century*. For documentation of the Cold War–era obsession with party membership, see the 118-page FBI file on Rukeyser (on the Web at http://foia.fbi.gov/rukeyser.htm), in which she is labeled a "concealed Communist," someone whom the bureau believed to be a Communist who would deny membership if asked directly. The term *concealed Communist* can be seen as the anti-Communist counterpart to Denning's wide net.

literary politics. . . . the times are much more dangerous than they were two years ago.[14]

Of course, deemphasizing the real intensity of conflict within the Left is an intrinsic hazard of Denning's quite worthwhile project. But for the purpose of understanding Muriel Rukeyser's political world, the fact that she met with Dupee in full knowledge of the serious, bitter conflict in which he was involved deserves emphasis, since it demonstrates that by the time she wrote *The Book of the Dead* she was working within the broad atmosphere of a Left of whose internal complexities she was aware.

On a more personal level, in September 1937 Rukeyser was only twenty-three, yet she already had to her credit a volume of poetry, *Theory of Flight*, issued as part of the prestigious Yale Younger Poets series in 1935. Rukeyser was widely seen as one of the most promising of a generation of poets emerging amid the social tensions and dislocations of the Great Depression. Although the reviews of *Theory of Flight* were not unstinting in their praise, the volume was, on the whole, favorably received, and Rukeyser was much encouraged. She wrote to Wheelwright: "My book is out, and having rather disturbing good luck, which makes me eager to get going, *really*, and is going to send me South in a few days to work on more"—that is, to research *The Book of the Dead*.[15]

Rukeyser was well prepared in many ways for the career that was just beginning. While a sudden dramatic downturn in her father's business forced her to leave Vassar after two years, her education was still very good. Born into a prosperous Jewish family in 1913, Rukeyser was educated at the Fieldston schools. These schools were associated with Ethical Culture, a quasi-religious movement that attempted to provide a comprehensive philosophy of life without recourse to the supernatural. The founder of the Ethical Culture movement, Felix Adler, was a significant influence on Rukeyser, according to her son, William Rukeyser,[16] and some elements of Adler's thought reappear, though transfigured, throughout her career.

Influenced by neo-Kantianism, Adler held the Kantian positions that the existence or nonexistence of a higher being cannot be drawn conclusively by pure reason and that morality can be established without theology. In

14. Gregory to Rukeyser, June 20, [1937], Gregory Papers. "Morris money" is a reference to George L. K. Morris, an artist and art critic for *Partisan Review*. Morris was from a wealthy family and financed the *Review* for the first few years after its revival.

15. Rukeyser to Wheelwright, March 1, 1936, Wheelwright Collection.

16. William Rukeyser, interview by author, Davis, Calif., June 5, 1995.

addition to Kant, Adler listed " 'Emerson' along with 'Jesus' and 'The He-
brew Religion' as formative influences." As Howard Radest notes, while
Adler would later play down the importance of Emerson to him, "Adler
was and remained far more Emersonian than he knew or admitted." In
addition, Adler was greatly interested in the social problems of his day,
in particular the problems posed by the development of a large industrial
working class. Radest writes that "[t]he labor question, Kant, and Emer-
son mingle with currents of the Jewish prophetic tradition and reform" in
Adler's work, a combination of elements that, while far from identical to
Rukeyser's, bears a real resemblance.[17]

More specifically, the conception of the artist in Adler's thought seems to
have made an impression on Rukeyser. In *An Ethical Philosophy of Life,* Adler
writes: "The vocation of the artist is to create the semblance of the spiri-
tual relation between the parts of an empirical object." That is, the artis-
tic function is to reveal the nonmaterial meanings that lie behind but also
pervade the things of this world. Adler goes on to say that the "spiritual
relation" may be produced in "any material which is capable of bearing
that imprint," a declaration of freedom that Rukeyser seems to have taken
to heart in her choice of poetic materials. Finally, the high-mindedness of
Adler's conception of the task of the artist clearly left its mark on Rukeyser:
"The relation of art . . . to the spiritual life . . . is to produce the semblance
of the spiritual relation, and thereby to rejuvenate the world's workers,
to give them the joy of relative perfection, and thus to stimulate them to
persevere in the real business of life, which is to approximate toward ac-
tual perfection."[18] The word *rejuvenate* might suggest that art functions in
a merely recreational manner for Adler, but it is probably more accurate to
emphasize the close relation between the form taken by this rejuvenation
and the role of art as a stimulus toward the goal of "actual perfection."
While I will suggest that Rukeyser's radically future-oriented vision, as
part of her politically radical utopian vision, ought to be understood pri-
marily in relation to the work of Ernst Bloch, Adler very likely helped to
set the pattern of this vision quite early.

More generally, from her background in the Ethical Culture movement
Rukeyser derived, at least in part, her inclination to see social develop-
ments in "spiritual" terms: that is, in terms of the effect of social conditions
on the possibility of the development of the full capacities of all human
beings. The movement sought to educate and uplift the people, and thus
to improve the world. Yet Rukeyser would also depart from Adler's Ethical
Culture. In intellectual terms, one can see this in Adler's rejection of Marx-
ism, which he objects to because of its materialism. For Adler, the workers'

17. Felix Adler, *An Ethical Philosophy of Life, Presented in Its Main Outlines,* 277, 282,
285; Howard Radest, prologue to *Felix Adler,* by Robert S. Guttchen, 23–24.
18. Adler, *Ethical Philosophy of Life,* 277, 282, 285.

movement ought not, as Marxism avers, ground itself in the real development of economic society, but in moral law.[19]

While deeply influenced by Ethical Culture's moral seriousness and desire to do good, Rukeyser came to realize that these characteristics, admirable enough in themselves, were products of class privilege. In her desire to escape the confines of that class privilege, she saw political leftism as both a logical extension of her background in Ethical Culture and the means by which to move beyond it. In this way, Rukeyser's personal development followed a path also traveled by other Americans. For example, the most important socialist publisher in the United States before the 1930s was Charles H. Kerr, who was raised within a liberal Unitarian tradition closely linked to the Ethical Culture movement.[20] Kerr was intellectually and emotionally grounded in a secularized version of a tradition of radical Protestantism whose great, though ambiguous, American luminary is Emerson but whose roots may be traced at least to the political-religious schisms of the English civil war. Although Rukeyser's background differed from Kerr's in its particulars, they shared a grounding in a largely secular, social reformist tradition whose radicalism was seriously limited by the class position on which it was based.

Rukeyser's desire to transcend the limits that her education—or rather her entire socialization—had imposed upon her is indicated by her reference in her letter to Wheelwright to her impending trip. In March 1936, several months before the trip that eventually took her to Spain, Rukeyser traveled to West Virginia with her friend Nancy Naumburg to research a poem she planned to write on the death of an unknown number of tunnel workers in the town of Gauley Bridge. In journeying to rural Appalachia, Rukeyser was continuing the education she elected to pursue in her youth after she "learned that people lived below Fifty-Seventh Street, below Fourteenth Street." Rukeyser's parents, for all their ministrations, did not bring her to know this broader world: "I learned that I had been brought up as a protected, blindfolded daughter."[21]

Though Rukeyser's trip to West Virginia was taken before her trip to Spain, the poem based on that trip was not written until she returned to the United States. It appears that Rukeyser began serious work on *The Book of the Dead* in the early summer of 1937, while she was living, briefly, in Los Angeles. She continued work on the poem throughout the fall, after her return to New York, and said in a postcard to Horace Gregory and his wife, Marya Zaturenska, near the end of October, "I must finish Gauley

19. Ibid., 44–47.
20. Allen Ruff, "*We Called Each Other Comrade*": *Charles H. Kerr & Company, Radical Publishers*, 1–55.
21. Muriel Rukeyser, *The Life of Poetry*, 220.

Bridge," her shorthand name for *The Book of the Dead*.[22] She must have finished the poem soon after she wrote the card, since *U.S. 1* was published in early 1938. The advent of the war in Spain, intervening between her trip to Gauley Bridge and the writing of the poem, encouraged her to see the events she investigated in West Virginia as a local instance of an unfolding global history.

Such a way of seeing, relating individual experiences and perceptions to transindividual developments and their meanings, was surely part of Rukeyser's method as an artist from the start, as may be seen from the first poem in *Theory of Flight*. In "Poem Out of Childhood" Rukeyser writes:

> Prinzip's year bore us : see us turning at breast
> quietly while the air throbs over Sarajevo
> after the mechanic laugh of that bullet.[23]

But Spain—especially "her" Spain, the Spain of Barcelona, July 1936—it seems, drove the lesson of interconnection home, pushing her to deepen this aspect of her work, so that exploring the not-always-obvious relations between things became central to her poetics. But before we can examine this, we must become acquainted with the events that sent Rukeyser to West Virginia in the first place.

The Gauley Tunnel Tragedy

On March 31, 1930, ground was broken in the construction of a three-mile-long tunnel beneath Gauley Mountain, in Fayette County, West Virginia. The tunnel was meant to divert part of the New River from its natural bed and channel it through a descent of 162 feet to a power station that would convert the force of the water into electric power. The electricity produced by the power station was in turn to be consumed in the nearby town of Boncar (later renamed Alloy) by a metallurgical plant that would also use the rock to be excavated during the construction of the tunnel. This rock was rich in silica, a compound essential to the production of an alloy used in the steel industry. So valuable was the silica that the tunnel's diameter was expanded, in ways extraneous to the flow of water through it, in order to extract more silica: the tunnel doubled as a mine. Behind both the hydroelectric project and the metallurgical plant stood one company, the

22. Rukeyser to Gregory and Zaturenska, October 24, 1937, Gregory Papers.
23. Muriel Rukeyser, *The Collected Poems of Muriel Rukeyser*, 4. All quotations from Rukeyser's poetry are from this edition unless specified otherwise and are cited parenthetically by page number.

Union Carbide and Carbon Corporation. For the construction of the tunnel through Gauley Mountain, Union Carbide entered on March 13, 1930, into a contract with the lowest of thirty-five bidders, the Rinehart and Dennis Company of Virginia, specifying that the tunnel be completed within two years, with economic penalties for failure to meet this deadline.[24]

If the construction of the tunnel involved what would become one of the country's best-known corporations, it also involved a small army of anonymous workers, many of them migrants, many black. According to a Union Carbide memorandum, 4,887 men were employed in the construction of the hydroelectric complex, of whom 2,982 worked at least some of the time in the tunnel itself. These workers, anxious for jobs in the early years of the Great Depression, had been alerted by word-of-mouth notice spread in part by agents employed by Rinehart and Dennis. News spread throughout the Southeast of work to be had on the New River hydroelectric project, and thousands of workers with no ties to the rural West Virginia community in which they were to work poured into Fayette County.[25]

The unorganized and transient nature of the workforce combined with the desire of Union Carbide and its associates for speed and economy in the construction of the tunnel to produce the greatest industrial disaster in the history of the United States. In an effort to save time and money—and to avoid penalties for late completion—Rinehart and Dennis, under the watchful eye of Union Carbide, used unsafe drilling practices, drilling "dry" rather than "wet"; dry drilling is faster than wet drilling, in which dust raised by drilling is washed out of the air by spraying water at the drill tip. In addition, Rinehart and Dennis provided inadequate ventilation, failed to issue protective respirators, and imposed subhuman living conditions upon the workers. As a result many workers developed acute silicosis, a disabling and ultimately fatal disease produced when silica dust is breathed into the lungs in sufficiently large quantity over a short period. Silica dust irritates the lung tissue, causing it to form fibrous growths that surround the intruding dust particles, eventually choking off the supply of oxygen to the body. Although it is difficult to say precisely how many workers died from silicosis in the Gauley Tunnel tragedy, the conservative estimate of Martin Cherniack in his 1986 book on the disaster, *The Hawk's Nest Incident*, is that 764 workers died from silicosis within five years of the completion of the tunnel.[26]

While Union Carbide ultimately stood behind the construction of the tunnel, the actual names and number of the parties involved is somewhat

24. Martin Cherniack, *The Hawk's Nest Incident: America's Worst Industrial Accident*, 12–16.
25. Ibid., 18.
26. Ibid., 89–105.

more complicated, which itself indicates the highly dubious nature of what was perpetrated in the mountains of West Virginia. The relationship between Union Carbide and Rinehart and Dennis was a simple contractual one between two independent firms, but it was the New Kanawha Power Company, a subsidiary of Union Carbide, that oversaw the construction of the hydroelectric complex. Licensed to build public utilities, the company was in fact "a legal fiction created by the parent company," whose top staff were important figures in Union Carbide, according to Cherniack. Despite being "a licensed public utility, its entire bounty was kept in private hands." The sole customer of the plant was Union Carbide. Behind the formation of the New Kanawha Power Company and the manipulation of its status was the desire to combine "solitary corporate control with minimal liability." Although it was a legal fiction, New Kanawha Power was a very real presence at the construction site. Union Carbide often operated through New Kanawha Power to plan the construction of the tunnel, set the terms on which the work would be done, and supervise the construction. New Kanawha Power was also responsible for the "medical care, safety precautions, ventilation, food, water, and housing" on the project.[27]

If New Kanawha Power was the subordinate offspring of Union Carbide, the Rinehart and Dennis Company was something like the hired man. Rinehart and Dennis was brought in as the lowest bidder to build the tunnel, and to do so under the conditions of a contract whose terms were set out by New Kanawha Power and ultimately by Union Carbide. New Kanawha Power staff made the major decisions, down to the choice of the types of equipment used on the job. Rinehart and Dennis, then, was merely honoring the terms of the contract it had signed when it ordered the men to practice dry drilling, and it relied upon New Kanawha Power, if indeed it occurred to the company to think much about it, to provide ventilation and to take other precautions to protect the health and safety of those who worked in the tunnel. Thus, any temptation to blame the small, obscure southern company, Rinehart and Dennis, and to absolve the big, sophisticated northern corporation, Union Carbide, should be resisted. This is a point that Cherniack explores in great detail and one that Rukeyser makes in a striking fashion in *The Book of the Dead* when she uses a Union Carbide stock quotation as a poetic line (97).

But can the employers in the Gauley Tunnel disaster rightly be held culpable? In the course of defending themselves against the various lawsuits brought against them, one of the arguments they made was that they were unaware of any danger to the workers from silica dust. They presented silicosis as a new phenomenon, or at least one newly discovered, and one they could not be held accountable for guarding against, given their inevitable

27. Ibid., 11, 16.

and blameless ignorance. However, as was made clear in testimony before a House subcommittee investigating the events at Gauley Bridge, the U.S. Department of Mines had been disseminating information about silicosis for twenty-five years before the construction of the tunnel. In addition, if Union Carbide had not anticipated some danger to its workforce, the question arises of why it was careful to recruit workers from outside the local community as opposed to concentrating on local workers, many of whom were experienced coal miners. Cherniack demonstrates that even though local workers were available to work on the project, "considerably less than 20 percent of the workers were local in origin." While the Gauley Tunnel tragedy did bring about the understanding that brief exposure to heavy concentrations of silica dust produces acute silicosis, as differentiated from classic, chronic silicosis, the basic disease was sufficiently understood before the tragedy to make the utter disregard for the exposure of tunnel workers to silica dust inexcusable.[28]

The inability of the tunnel workers to resist the abuses inflicted by their employers may in part be explained by the nature of the workforce. To drive the tunnel through more than three miles of solid rock, a workforce was assembled that was largely though not exclusively migrant in character. As noted, fewer than 20 percent of the men who worked inside the tunnel—the only place where dust concentrations made silicosis a danger—were locals, according to Union Carbide's records. Most of these migrant workers were black. As a result, the majority (around 75 percent) of workers inside the tunnel were black. By recruiting black laborers into mostly (80 percent) white Fayette County, the employers sought to ensure some distance between the tunnel workforce and the local population. This plan worked to a great extent. Evidence that the unhealthy conditions inside the tunnel were killing the workers was compelling; yet, in certain sectors of the local population, the blame was placed on the careless living habits of the black workers, who, as the undertaker Hadley C. White in *The Book of the Dead* says:

> got wet at work,
> shot craps, drank and took cold, pneumonia, died. (89)

The death toll from the tunnel was thus often explained away as resulting from poor "lifestyle choices" rather than as the product of a number of economically driven choices made by Rinehart and Dennis, New Kanawha Power, and Union Carbide.[29]

28. Ibid., 55–67, 17, 37–40.
29. Ibid., 17–18, 52–53. In fairness, it should be noted that the local juries who heard the lawsuits brought against employers tended to be sympathetic to the worker-plain-

News of the disaster in remote West Virginia spread slowly, and, by the very nature of the case, rumor and speculation mixed liberally with fact. The tunnel had been completed for over three years and lawsuits had been filed on behalf of stricken workers for more than two years before *New Masses* ran several pieces in 1935 describing the man-made disaster.[30] Several other publications, including the Detroit labor paper, the *People's Press,* followed the lead of *New Masses,* and the disaster came to the attention of the U.S. House of Representatives at the urging of Rep. Vito Marcantonio, a member of the Committee on Labor.[31] Marcantonio served on a subcommittee that held hearings on the events in Fayette County, and while the subcommittee's request in 1936 for funding and the power of subpoena in order to conduct an investigation was denied, by the end of 1937 legislation protecting workers from silicosis had been passed in forty-six states. This legislation, according to Cherniack, was made possible by the heightened awareness of the threat of silicosis produced by the hearings.[32]

The hearings received extensive coverage when they were held in January and February of 1936. The *Daily Worker* ran Gauley Tunnel–related articles on a nearly daily basis during the hearings, as well as a political cartoon by William Gropper captioned "Murder in Gauley's [*sic*] Bridge" (January 20, 1936) and a photograph of George Robison, Charles Jones, and Emma Jones, all of whom had testified before the House subcommittee and all of whom figure in *The Book of the Dead* (January 28, 1936). The *Daily Worker* also published a poem in ballad form, "Silicosis in Our Town," by Martha Millet (June 2, 1936) that, like *The Book of the Dead,* relied heavily on testimony delivered before the House subcommittee (see Appendix I).[33] More than half a decade after work on the tunnel began, and due almost

---

tiffs. However, a variety of factors, including jury-tampering by the employers, honest doubt and confusion on the part of jurors, and employer-friendly judges, resulted in hung juries in the two cases that were fully adjudicated (52–65).

30. Philippa Allen [Bernard Allen, pseud.], "Two Thousand Dying on a Job"; Albert Maltz, "Man on a Road"; Cherniack, *Hawk's Nest Incident,* 75.

31. Marcantonio began his political career as a protégé of Fiorello La Guardia, the liberal, reformist Republican mayor of New York City (the Republicans served as an alternative to the corrupt Tammany Hall Democrats). Serving in the House of Representatives from 1935 to 1937 and from 1939 to 1950, Marcantonio was considerably more radical than La Guardia. After breaking his ties with the Republicans and failing to be reelected in 1936, he ran on the leftist American Labor Party ticket from 1938 until his defeat in 1950. A consistent advocate of civil rights and working-class interests, Marcantonio was one of the most successful left-wing politicians in American history. See Alan Schaffer, *Vito Marcantonio, Radical in Congress,* 11–65.

32. Cherniack, *Hawk's Nest Incident,* 79, 110.

33. Unlike Rukeyser, Millet does not incorporate the transcript of the hearings into her poem, but rather uses it as background information around which she constructs her ballad. Like Rukeyser, Millet puts the story of the Jones family at the center of her poem. Millet, however, ranges far from the immediate concerns of Rukeyser's poem based on the Joneses, "Absalom." Overall, *The Book of the Dead* is a far more ambitious poem both thematically and formally. Because it uses the ballad form, Millet's poem

wholly to the efforts of the Left, the disaster at Gauley Bridge entered into public consciousness.

The Method of *The Book of the Dead*

The scenario I have described might suggest that instead of writing a poem about the Gauley Tunnel tragedy, Rukeyser should have left the incident to the journalists, or turned journalist herself. And so judged some of her reviewers. But Rukeyser produced a *poem* out of this tragedy, seeing in it a complex of the warring forces, tendencies, and possibilities in human history. In so doing, she forfeited some of the advantages of journalism (immediacy of impact, accessibility, and the presumption of objectivity) in favor of some of the advantages of poetry (a richness and density of texture, which enables a more challenging and searching treatment of the subject).[34] The point is not that poetry is better or worse than journalism, but rather that, while it shares with journalism many features, poetry also lacks some features of journalism and enjoys some virtues distinctive to it.

While Rukeyser had recourse to all the potentialities of poetic discourse, *The Book of the Dead* challenges any poetics that removes poetry from the ugliness and conflict of the real world of labor and politics. In one sense, inclusion of the ugly and unpleasant simply follows from Rukeyser's commitment to poetic modernism as a reaction against the vapid poeticizing of the Genteel Tradition.[35] But Rukeyser also positions *The Book of the Dead* against contemporary aesthetes for whom Gauley Bridge stands outside the proper realm of the poetic:

> What do you want—a cliff over a city?
> A foreland, sloped to sea and overgrown with roses?
> These people live here.   (76)

Rukeyser elaborated upon this sentiment shortly after the publication of *U.S. 1* when, in her radio interview with Samuel Sillen, she stated her desire

---

speaks directly to the folk-song tradition that was being made available to a wider public in the 1920s and 1930s, most significantly in this case in the work of George Korson, whose books included *Songs and Ballads of the Anthracite Miner* (1927). Rukeyser was aware of this tradition; "George Robinson: Blues" is one indication of this. In *The Life of Poetry* (1949), she refers to a "barroom ballad" called "Down, Down, Down," the lyrics to which Korson published in *Minstrels of the Mine Patch* (1938) and a field recording of which he released in 1947. While it is difficult to assert anything definite, Rukeyser was attuned to this kind of material.

34. In *From Fact to Fiction: Journalism and Imaginative Writing in America,* Shelley Fisher Fishkin claims that the desire to go beyond journalism without abandoning its claims to truth is a crucial component in much American writing.

35. For a valuable treatment of the relationship between modernism and the Genteel Tradition, see Frank Lentricchia, *Modernist Quartet.*

to bring poetry into contact with the broad range of human experience. Much of the interview focused on *The Book of the Dead*, and in the course of their discussion Sillen drew from Rukeyser a deceptively illuminating response:

> **Sillen:** Isn't this an unusual theme for poetry, Miss Rukeyser? Most people associate poetry with what they call the pleasant things in life. How would you justify the use of such a theme as you have selected?
>
> **Rukeyser:** I feel that it is on material of this sort that poetry must now build itself, as well as on those personal responses which have always been the basis for poetry. The actual world, not some fantastic structure that has nothing to do with reality, must provide the material for modern poetry.[36]

Rukeyser might have been defending the practice of a politically committed literature that works from social reality as opposed to an aestheticist or formalist conception of literature that values distance from political commitment and social reality. But she might also have been commenting on the practice of modern poetry in general. As a growing body of scholarship attests, these are not contradictory options, whatever the practical difficulties posed by the competing demands of politics and modernism.[37] Thus Rukeyser affirmed both political commitment and the basic tenets of modernist poetry. (See Appendix III for the complete interview.)

That Rukeyser wanted to write a poetry based upon both "the actual world, not some fantastic structure," and "those personal responses which have always been the basis for poetry" proves crucial to her project in *The Book of the Dead*. In her formulation, subject and object keep their distance from one another; their nonidentity is recognized. This nonidentity of subject and object underpins *The Book of the Dead* both thematically and formally.

Thematically, the poem confronts what is arguably the fundamental problem of modernist poetry: the rift between subjective meaning, the importance that one ascribes to something as an individual, and objective values, the importance that one's society ascribes to something. This rift is paralleled by another: the one between values, whether those of individual or collective subjects, and reality, whether understood as "society" or

36. Muriel Rukeyser, radio interview by Samuel Sillen, transcript, [1938], Berg Collection, New York Public Library.

37. Out of the substantial and growing body of work on politics and modernism in American literature, most relevant to the concerns of this chapter are Alan Wald, *The Revolutionary Imagination: The Poetry and Politics of John Wheelwright and Sherry Mangan*; Cary Nelson, *Repression and Recovery: Modern American Poetry and the Politics of Cultural Memory, 1910–1945*; and Alan Filreis, *Modernism from Right to Left: Wallace Stevens, the Thirties, and Literary Radicalism*.

as brute nature.[38] This second rift is embodied in *The Book of the Dead* in the apparently meaningless and irredeemable deaths of the tunnel workers. At first glance these deaths seem to refuse meaning and to have no place in any greater system of value. They resemble the deaths described by Frederic Henry in *A Farewell to Arms*: "sacrifices . . . like the stockyards at Chicago if nothing was done with the meat except to bury it."[39] That is, in a capitalist modern world stripped of a transcendent, meaning-giving framework such as that provided the feudal Middle Ages by Roman Catholicism, they remain merely the affairs of isolate subjects and do not register in the world of either social or natural objectivity as anything more than statistics, if they register at all; the deaths are, initially, pure negations. Rukeyser's thematic concern with redeeming that negativity finds a formal counterpart in the variety of poetic modes she employs in *The Book of the Dead*.

My argument comes down to this: in order to get at what Rukeyser was attempting to do with and in *The Book of the Dead*, one needs to see the poem as composed of basic generic elements that serve distinctive functions within the poem as a whole. These basic elements, I argue, may be understood through the traditional tripartite analysis of the genres: lyric, epic, and dramatic, though one needs to be aware that these elements are typically found intermixed in the poem and that the distinctions I make are of an analytical character. In any case, the various genres perform distinct functions in the poem.

The poems that are primarily lyrical in character register the immediately subjective dimension of the disaster: the impact that this catastrophe had upon the individual lives affected by it. The lyrical poems explore the "interior" dimensions of the Gauley Tunnel tragedy, a disaster that claimed primarily people whose social status, because of their class and/or race, differentiates them from the typical lyrical subject. Thus the lyrical poems register a dimension of the disaster that is lost if it is apprehended purely in terms of the "facts of the matter," at the same time that they give poetic speech to people ordinarily denied such speech.

The poems that I consider in terms of the characteristics of the epic might more conventionally (and certainly not inaccurately) be described as documentary. In these poems, which she works up from decidedly nonpoetic

---

38. While a description of this problem may be found in a number of places, I prefer that in Franco Moretti, "From *The Waste Land* to the Artificial Paradise," for its clarity and its resonance in a variety of fields other than literature (210–18). Among those who have discussed the topic, Robert Langbaum has also stated the case with admirable concision and clarity (*The Poetry of Experience: The Dramatic Monologue in Modern Literary Tradition*). However, his stress upon the continuity between nineteenth- and twentieth-century literature leads him to overlook the distinctions that Moretti makes clear. In particular, the disappearance of nature as a realm of transcendent values would seem to separate decisively the modernists from the romantics.

39. Ernest Hemingway, *A Farewell to Arms*, 185.

texts, Rukeyser registers the objective dimensions of the Gauley Tunnel tragedy: the basic who, what, where, and when of the case at hand. In these poems Rukeyser faced the challenge of integrating into the larger poem a fairly large amount of factual information. Given that the dominant understanding of poetry as it had developed into the early twentieth century made "fact" into that which was quite nearly an opposite to "poetry," the challenge was considerable.

Finally, a cluster of four poems in *The Book of the Dead* is of a dramatic character. In characterizing these poems as dramatic, I do not refer to their superficial form, but rather to the purpose they play in the larger poem's structure. These poems are essentially reflections or meditations on the meaning of the Gauley Tunnel tragedy, not in terms of any individual experience of it, but rather in terms of the unfolding history of humanity. The dramatic character of the poems emerges from the fundamentally conflictual nature of the history that Rukeyser sees concentrated within the disaster.

However central the generic analysis I have just outlined may be, it forms only one strand of my argument. The other major strand derives from the utopian nature of Rukeyser's vision. This vision may be seen in a few lines from an early Rukeyser poem, "This House, This Country." In the poem the speaker reflects upon her relationship with her family, who look with disapproval and fear upon the life she has chosen:

> Over my shoulder
> I see they grow older
> their vision fails : observe I travel light
> fear distance hope I shall only spend the night.
>
> But night in this country
> is deep promise of day   (20)

In the last two lines, the negative is taken as a sign of its opposite, and such an ability to see, or to search for, the bases for hope is fundamental to Rukeyser's poetics. It is for this reason that *The Book of the Dead* may—or, as I argue, must—be read in terms of Ernst Bloch's utopian poetics: the negative is susceptible to analysis in terms of its opposite.

Something like this kind of logic guides Rukeyser's use of the Egyptian *Book of the Dead* as a predecessor, of sorts, to her poem.[40] The Egyptian

---

40. Rukeyser had seen the Egyptian *Book of the Dead* at the British Museum during her visit to England in the summer of 1936; Rukeyser to Marya Zaturenska, June 25, 1936, Gregory Papers. Also, in the course of a very critical and condescending letter, a Miss Laura Abel of the National League of American Pen Women mentions the Egyptian *Book of the Dead*; Abel to Rukeyser, January 26, 1936, Rukeyser Papers.

Book of the Dead is a collection of sacred texts that were placed in coffins beginning around the fifteenth century B.C. It was intended to serve the deceased as a guide to the afterlife and was composed of about two hundred chapters, a variable number of which might be contained in any particular text—the Egyptian *Book of the Dead* was never standardized, was never a "book," properly speaking. While Rukeyser uses the title of and quotations from the Egyptian *Book of the Dead*, she does not pattern her poem extensively after its precursor. Still, she carries over several primary elements from it. They are: (1) some geography, (2) a concern with the moral status of the dead, and (3) a conception of resurrection.[41]

An important point of contact between the Egyptian and Rukeyser's *Book of the Dead* is geography. A crucial feature of the Egyptian underworld was water. Water pervaded the underworld, representing and embodying the primordial chaos out of which the ordered world sprang but which persisted after the world's creation. These waters also had a rejuvenating quality, and thus were characterized by both negative and positive qualities. Similarly, the river whose water is central to Rukeyser's poem is both "the river Death" and a source and symbol of life.[42] It may be that this kind of duality, characteristic of ancient Egyptian religious thought, is partly what recommended to Rukeyser the use of the Egyptian precursor text.

Like the primordial waters, the underworld, or *Duat*, had a dual character: it was the home of Osiris, the chief god of rebirth; yet it was also the home of Seth, the chief enemy of Osiris, as well as the home of a variety of beings who "were inimical not only to the deceased, but to Osiris as well."[43] Similarly, Rukeyser's subterranean world, her underworld, is a place of death but also of life, because in her conception the construction of the tunnel is linked on a deep level with a truly human power. Again, it may be that the duality of the original Egyptian conception, the internally related nature of the positive and the negative, is what appealed to Rukeyser's imagination, since it functioned in a manner she found familiar and congenial.

A fundamental feature of the Egyptian conception of the afterlife is the judgment of the dead. While the Egyptian *Book of the Dead* instructed the deceased in various means of defeating the irrational forces of the underworld that threaten the innocent without regard to their righteousness, belief in the judgment of the dead added a profound moral element to the Egyptian conception of the afterlife. Rukeyser may have been influenced

41. For more on the relationship between Rukeyser's poem and the Egyptian text, see Philip Blair Rice, "The Osiris Way"; M. L. Rosenthal, "The Longer Poems of Muriel Rukeyser"; David Kadlec, "X-Ray Testimonials in Muriel Rukeyser."

42. Ogden Goelet, ed., *The Egyptian Book of the Dead: The Book of Going Forth by Day*, 143.

43. Ibid., 143.

by the conception of Egyptian religion found in James Henry Breasted's *The Dawn of Conscience*, published in 1934, shortly before she began work on *The Book of the Dead*. Certainly there are elements of Breasted's interpretation of the development of Egyptian culture that would have appealed to her, and the book was in the catalog of the New York Public Library, where Rukeyser did research for *The Book of the Dead*.

Breasted placed his argument concerning the "dawn of conscience" in ancient Egypt squarely within the post–World War I sense of crisis: conscience, Breasted felt, was the only force capable of countering the destructive power that technology had attained and which was demonstrated in that war. Breasted presented the emergence of ethics and the notion of righteousness as an historical and social phenomenon, not as the product of revelation: "It was a result of the social experience of *man himself* and was not projected into the world from the outside." This fact—that of social evolution at the level of thought—was the occasion for a degree of optimism not altogether characteristic of the interwar period. For Breasted, the emergence of conscience—"[n]ot projected from the outside into a world of unworthy men by some mystic process called inspiration or revelation, but springing out of man's own life two thousand years before the theologians' 'age of revelation' began, illuminating the darkness of social disillusionment and inner conflict"—provided "a glorious vindication of the worth of man."[44]

Interestingly, Breasted saw the Egyptian *Book of the Dead* as countering the trend toward "the dawn of conscience" because it represented an attempt to use magical incantations as protections for the deceased, regardless of the degree to which they were or were not among the righteous: "In so far as The Book of the Dead had become a magical agency for securing moral vindication in the hereafter, irrespective of character, it had become a positive force for evil." However, because *The Book of the Dead* also contained the notion that righteousness concerns something beyond mere compliance with the obligatory rituals of religion, it retained value in "its elaboration of the ancient idea of the moral judgment, and its evident appreciation of the burden of conscience."[45] This concern with the moral judgment of the dead based upon the behavior of individuals in their earthly existence—one of Breasted's points of evidence—obviously appealed to Rukeyser.

The place where the Egyptian conception of individual judgment enters most directly into the poem is in the lyrical monologue "Absalom," in which Rukeyser adapts a passage from the Egyptian *Book of the Dead*.

44. James Henry Breasted, *The Dawn of Conscience*, xv, xvi.
45. Ibid., 265, 270.

According to the E. A. Wallis Budge translation on which Rukeyser relied, when the judgment of the deceased is being made, he is proclaimed to be one "whose word is true" and "who is holy and righteous."[46] Rukeyser transferred this idea to one of the tunnel workers who has died from silicosis, Shirley Jones. Shirley is judged to be innocent and to have been wronged. Yet judgment in the Rukeyser version of *The Book of the Dead* will not fall on individuals so much as it will on groups and classes.

Closely linked to the question of judgment is the third element that Rukeyser carried over from Egyptian religion and the *Book of the Dead:* the concept of rebirth or resurrection. Again, a key moment occurs in "Absalom," when Shirley is granted the power to *"journey over the earth among the living"* (83). And again, this element found at the level of the individual will return at the level of the transindividual or the collective. In "The Dam" the history of the working class is figured according to terms whereby Rukeyser can conclude: "It changes. It does not die" (98). As with the idea of rebirth, she refunctions the notion of judgment in Egyptian religion for her different purposes in *The Book of the Dead:* rebirth and judgment become figurative and, ultimately, collective rather than literal and individual.

Rukeyser's poem, however, *builds* to this collective, transindividual level, beginning largely with poems that are either lyrical in character, presenting a slice of reality as it is perceived and experienced by a particular individual, or documentary in character, presenting the world within which these individual perceptions and experiences were formed. Only after these two levels have been firmly established does the poem move on to the collective dimension, in what I term the meditative section of *The Book of the Dead.* This progression structures the heart of this study, chapters 2 through 4. In Chapter 2, I examine the opening of the poem and the establishment of the lyrical perspectives on the Gauley Tunnel tragedy. In Chapter 3, I shift to the documentary sections of the poem, emphasizing their role in establishing the objective circumstances surrounding the tragedy. In Chapter 4, I move on to the meditative sequence and the poem's synthetic conclusion.

Below is a schematic presentation of the ordering of the poems as they appear in *The Book of the Dead* compared to the ordering of the poems as I consider them. *The Book of the Dead* was published with its constituent poems in the sequence shown in the left-hand column; I rearrange them into the sequence in the right-hand column (listed under the headings, in boldface, by which I organize them):

46. E. A. Wallis Budge, ed. and trans., *The Egyptian Book of the Dead*, 373.

	Introductory Poems
"The Road"	"The Road"
"West Virginia"	"West Virginia"
"Statement: Philippa Allen"	"Statement: Philippa Allen"
"Gauley Bridge"	"Gauley Bridge"
	Lyrical Monologues
"The Face of the Dam: Vivian Jones"	"The Face of the Dam: Vivian Jones"
"Praise of the Committee"	"Mearl Blankenship"
"Mearl Blankenship"	"Absalom"
"Absalom"	"George Robinson: Blues"
"The Disease"	"Juanita Tinsley"
"George Robinson: Blues"	"Arthur Peyton"
	Documentary Poems
"Juanita Tinsley"	"Praise of the Committee"
"The Doctors"	"The Disease"
"The Cornfield"	"The Doctors"
"Arthur Peyton"	"The Disease: After-Effects"
"Alloy"	"The Bill"
	Meditations
"Power"	"The Cornfield"
"The Dam"	"Alloy"
"The Disease: After-Effects"	"Power"
"The Bill"	"The Dam"
	Coda
"The Book of the Dead"	"The Book of the Dead"

My analytical reconstruction of the poem differs from the poem itself primarily in regard to the documentary poems, which are more widely distributed throughout the longer poem than my abstraction would suggest. Still, while an even greater divergence from the actual sequence of the poems as Rukeyser presented them would be perfectly justifiable, in my opinion, I am faithful to the general trend of *The Book of the Dead*.

While chapters 2–4, outlined above, are primarily concerned with close readings, the two chapters that follow expand the framework within which I consider Rukeyser's poem. Chapter 5 looks at the critical reception of the poem, starting with Rukeyser's contemporaries and moving up to the present day. The concluding chapter makes explicit several arguments which bubble under the previous chapters, presents the Marxist theoretical-critical framework within which my reading of Rukeyser has been conducted, and argues briefly for the continued vitality of Marxism in literary and cultural study as we begin a new millennium. Since, as I will argue, a Marxist theory of history underpins *The Book of the Dead*, I will not range so far from my original object of study as it may appear. At least, I hope not—but that is ultimately for the reader to decide.

2

Introductory Poems
and Lyrical Monologues

Introductory Poems

In the first four poems of *The Book of the Dead*, "The Road," "West Virginia," "Statement: Philippa Allen," and "Gauley Bridge," Rukeyser establishes the primary voice through which the poem will be delivered, the setting in which it will take place, and the events with which it will be concerned. She also establishes the modes that will dominate the first half of the poem: the lyrical and the documentary. The poems are thus introductory in terms of both content and form: they inform the reader about the topic of the poem and they alert the reader to the sometimes demanding nature of the long poem that he or she has undertaken to read.

Written in twelve unrhymed, three-line stanzas, "The Road" opens *The Book of the Dead* by emphasizing its nature as a journey. Rukeyser does this not only by means of the poem's title and content, but also by producing a strong sense of sequential unfolding through the use of fixed stanzas at the beginning and end of the poem.[1] This permits a logical tautness usually associated with narrative in this non-narrative poem. Seven stanzas (1–3, 5–6, 11–12) are part of open stanzaic constructions, while five are closed, lending to the poem a sense of movement, openness, and development, without creating a sense of headlong rush, but rather of deliberate, considered movement. "The Road" opens *The Book of the Dead* by characterizing the poem's journey as the result of careful forethought:

---

1. In referring to "fixed" stanzas, I use the terminology found in Ernst Häublein, *The Stanza*. Fixed stanzas are those whose order may not be altered without affecting the sense or meaning of the poem. Those stanzas which may be reordered Häublein refers to as "exchangeable."

These are roads to take when you think of your country
and interested bring down the maps again,
phoning the statistician, asking the dear friend,

reading the papers with morning inquiry.   (71)

These opening lines also establish the sequential refrain (that is, a refrain with variations) of *The Book of the Dead:* "These are roads to take . . ."

This refrain, as well as Rukeyser's general affiliation, critical though it is, with the Whitmanian tradition, suggest that "The Road" is a kind of updating and revision of Whitman's "Song of the Open Road." Whitman's poem uses a device similar to "These are roads," in the anaphoric lines beginning "Here is . . . ," as in: "Here is a man tallied—he realizes here what he has in him."[2] Rukeyser's poem stands in a relationship of difference-within-similarity with Whitman's: both are "road" poems, and both conceive of the journey undertaken as providing an occasion for the self to encounter and be impressed by a world that stands witness:

You windows whose transparent shells might expose so much!
You doors and ascending steps! you arches!
You gray stones of interminable pavements! you trodden crossings!
From all that has touch'd you I believe you have imparted to yourselves,
    and now would impart the same secretly to me,
From the living and the dead you have peopled your impassive surfaces,
    and the spirits thereof would be evident and amicable with me.[3]

The underlying spirit of the journey is consistent from Whitman to Rukeyser and, as William Stott points out, to many other writers in the 1930s as well who prized the capacities of the Whitmanian " 'I'—able to see, incorporate, and give voice to all human experience. . . . Whitman's stance of *being there* was a criterion of authenticity in expression at the time."[4] Both poems insist on the importance of the encounter between the spiritual or mental realm, with which poetry is all-too-readily identified, and the physical world of material reality.

---

2. Walt Whitman, "Song of the Open Road," in *Leaves of Grass: Comprehensive Reader's Edition*, 149–59, line 86.

3. Ibid., lines 34–38.

4. William Stott, *Documentary Expression and Thirties America*, 36. The Whitmanian urge to go on the road was shared by a great number of Rukeyser's contemporaries in the 1930s, as is pointed out by Stott and by David P. Peeler in "Unlonesome Highways: The Quest for Fact and Fellowship in Depression America." Stott comments that "looking for America" was a common theme in the 1930s. Previous treatments of this theme were metaphorical; writers in the '30s took the metaphor and made it literal: they went "on the road" (241).

"Song of the Open Road" is what is thought of as typically Whitmanian: the dominant tone is confident and optimistic. The world lies waiting for the self to take possession of it:

> Afoot and light-hearted I take to the open road,
> Healthy, free, the world before me,
> The long brown path before me leading wherever I choose.[5]

The difference between this beginning and that of Rukeyser's poem points to the physical, material difference between the mid-nineteenth- and mid-twentieth-century United States, but also to the intellectual difference between Whitman's largely romantic and Rukeyser's postromantic outlook.[6] Whitman's confident, capacious self determines its journey, while Rukeyser's speaker presents the journey as one into a world that more likely determines the self; or, alternatively, the self willingly makes itself subject to the outside world, in an encounter which will change it.

Furthermore, Rukeyser's is a world not immediately available. This contrast informs the difference between Whitman's line "Let the paper remain on the desk unwritten, and the book on the shelf unopened!"[7] and Rukeyser's lines quoted above, where one will "interested bring down the maps again, / phoning the statistician, asking the dear friend, // reading the papers with morning inquiry." Whereas in Whitman spontaneity rules, in Rukeyser's poem the speaker has some research to do before setting out,

---

5. Whitman, "Song of the Open Road," lines 1–3.

6. In *Willard Gibbs* (1942), Rukeyser depicts Whitman as more friendly to science, and thus less romantic, than seems warranted. She might be seen as producing a Whitman who, as one founder of the American poetic tradition, is more conformable to her own branch of that tradition than the actual Whitman, in all his famous self-contradictoriness, was. Robert J. Scholnick, too, argues that Whitman was in fact more open to and influenced by contemporary science than is traditionally assumed (" 'The Password Primeval': Whitman's Use of Science in *Song of Myself*," 385–86). The crucial distinction here concerns the nature of the enthusiasm for science that Scholnick documents. Whitman's embrace of the discoveries of nineteenth-century science seems to be of a piece with his celebration of technological advances in "Passage to India" and to concern primarily discoveries conformable with an optimistic (if also at times ambivalent) nineteenth-century view of progress, rather than an embrace of scientific method— although it should be acknowledged that he praised "[e]xact science and its practical movements" in the 1855 preface to *Leaves of Grass* (*Comprehensive Reader's Edition*, 718). In "When I Heard the Learned Astronomer" Whitman rejects a form of knowledge that does not experientially replicate its object, in favor of a supposed immediate identification of the knower and the known in a spontaneous encounter with the cosmos. This tendency toward identification, with its collapse of ontology into epistemology, I would argue, predominates in Whitman. Rukeyser writes that Whitman "said continually, 'Identify.' " She contrasts Whitman's stance in this regard with that of the scientist Gibbs, who said, "I wish to know systems" (*Willard Gibbs*, 358, 4).

7. Whitman, "Song of the Open Road," l. 216.

and the world and its meanings are not immediately accessible to intuition or casual observation.

Beginning *The Book of the Dead* with "The Road" was both a statement of affiliation with Whitman and his America as exemplified in "Song of the Open Road" and a corrective to it, constructed in light of historical experience and new knowledge. Both Rukeyser's and Whitman's poems present versions of the traditional lyrical form, the *chanson d'aventure*, in which a physical journey leads to a spiritual ("Song of the Open Road") or an intellectual and emotional (*The Book of the Dead*) discovery. But where Whitman constructs a poem that "for all its seeming tangibleness . . . is decidedly a personal vision" in which "the poet-persona filters what he sees through the self rather than through any broader objective context,"[8] Rukeyser's poem attempts to mediate between the objective and subjective worlds in a way that does not collapse one into the other.

Accordingly, she carefully presents the journey of "The Road" as one that moves both outward and inward. This double movement is indicated by the sequential refrain that she establishes. Thus the refrain that first appears in an objectively-oriented form, "These are roads to take when you think of your country," reappears in a more subjectively oriented form: "These roads will take you into your own country" (71). This country is simultaneously physical, one through which we move and to which we are rejoined in the course of the journey, and mental, as the journey forces us to place ourselves in relation to that which will be revealed.

Physically, "The Road" takes us into West Virginia, where

> the Midland Trail leaves the Virginia furnace,
> iron Clifton Forge, Covington iron, goes down
> into the wealthy valley, resorts, the chalk hotel.
>
> Pillars and fairway; spa; White Sulphur Springs.
> Airport. Gay blank rich faces wishing to add
> history to ballrooms, tradition to the first tee. (71)

In these lines Rukeyser establishes the speaker's partisanship by employing an irony reminiscent of her acquaintance and contemporary Kenneth Fearing.[9] A different sort of irony underlies the juxtaposition of the relatively domesticated world within whose orbit the poet ordinarily lives

---

8. Harold Aspiz, "Whitman's 'Poem of the Road,'" 171.

9. Rukeyser clearly respected Fearing's poetry, but was very aware of its limitations and wanted to be a poet less restricted than she felt Fearing to be. In the summer of 1938, while she was in residence at Yaddo, an artist's retreat in Saratoga, New York, Rukeyser wrote about Fearing to Horace Gregory and Marya Zaturenska: "The one tune is a good one, of course, but he can't move in its limits, and he can't, at the moment, break them. I like his work very much, but up here, seeing him around, he's so

and the world she is about to enter: she drives on a "well-travelled six-lane highway planned for safety" (71) that contrasts sharply with the conditions in which, as the reader is about to see, the tunnel workers labored. This irony darkens the tone of "The Road"; Rukeyser's world is less benevolently disposed, less inclined toward amelioration than is Whitman's, and her stance is more openly political as a result.

In the final lines of "The Road" Rukeyser establishes the centrality of the New River, around which the action of the poem revolves and to which she will constantly return:

> Here is your road, tying
>
> you to its meanings: gorge, boulder, precipice.
> Telescoped down, the hard and stone-green river
> cutting fast and direct into the town.   (72)

The Book of the Dead is to be an exploration of "meanings," a journey that will throw the traveler into an encounter with a reality often apparently barren and sometimes worse. But only through this journey, and the interaction of subject and object it entails, is meaning to be discovered. These last lines achieve a closure suited to the first poem of a larger poetic construction. With, as Robert Shulman notes, a deft use of the internal rhyme of "down" and "town," we are delivered to the scene with which *The Book of the Dead* will be concerned.[10]

The physical journey begun in "The Road" becomes temporal in "West Virginia," a poem that takes the reader into the historical, as well as the spatial, dimension. To accomplish this, Rukeyser employs a roughly documentary mode and shifts to a less-personal voice. She begins by drawing upon early accounts of the exploration of the Alleghenies and the European discovery of the area around Gauley Bridge, carefully recreating the sense of excitement generated by the discovery:

> They saw rivers flow west and hoped again.
> Virginia speeding to another sea!
> 1671—Thomas Batts, Robert Fallam,
> Thomas Wood, the Indian Perecute,

---

much living model of a person who doesn't value his craft enough and is getting stuck because of it—he makes me want to experiment and learn and plan ahead against that chance" (n.d., Gregory Papers). This concern about developing a command of poetic technique, and that political concerns and consciousness not become a substitute for it, runs throughout Rukeyser's correspondence of the 1930s and 1940s, especially with Zaturenska and Gregory.

10. Robert Shulman, *The Power of Political Art: The 1930s Literary Left Reconsidered*, 187.

and an unnamed indentured English servant
followed the forest past blazed trees, pillars of God,
were the first whites emergent from the east.   (72)

Rukeyser worked this section up from a locally published history, Phil Conley's *West Virginia Yesterday and Today*.[11] She reproduces the sense of excitement and wonder—never far removed from utopian longings—common in the literature of exploration and discovery and which finds renewed expression in Crèvecoeur, Jefferson, Paine, and others who envision America as the place where the problems of Europe will be solved, or simply avoided.

"West Virginia" is primarily factual,[12] although the facts present a particular—though hardly idiosyncratic—interpretation of West Virginia as

War-born:
The battle at Point Pleasant, Cornstalk's tribes,
last stand, Fort Henry, a revolution won   (72)

The history of West Virginia that Rukeyser presents is extremely condensed and requires explanation: "The battle at Point Pleasant" took place on October 10, 1774, at the confluence of the Kanawha River (into which the New River flows) and the Ohio River. Fought between Virginia colonial militia and a combined force of Shawnee, Mingo, Wyandotte, Delaware, and Cayuga warriors, it was recognized as the first battle of the American Revolution by an act of the Sixtieth Congress in 1907. (Relations between the Virginia colonists and Lord Dunmore, the Royal Governor of Virginia, had greatly deteriorated by the fall of 1774, and Dunmore may have intentionally provoked war with the Indians and then withheld military support at Point Pleasant so that the Virginians would be crushed.) Cornstalk was the leader of the Shawnee forces in the battle. The Shawnee felt that it was their last opportunity to stop the colonialists' expansion into their lands, hence their "last stand." "Fort Henry, a revolution won" refers to the last major battle of the revolution, fought at the site of present-day Wheeling, West Virginia, in September 1782.[13]

Even here, in the early days of America, the picture Rukeyser draws is not without shadows. The utopia of the New World stands under two

11. A page of notes in Rukeyser's handwriting on West Virginia history is headed *"The Book of the Dead"* and is followed by the publication information for Conley's book (Rukeyser Papers).

12. Rukeyser appears to have worked primarily from Conley, *West Virginia*, 72–74, 94, 98.

13. E. Lee North, *Redcoats, Redskins, and Red-eyed Monsters*, 43–48, 55–58; John E. Selby, *The Revolution in Virginia, 1775–1783*, 17.

clouds in "West Virginia": the oppressions that accompanied discovery and exploration, and the poet's knowledge of the history that was to unfold, such as the tragedy of the collision of Europeans and native Americans. Thus Rukeyser mentions "the Indian Perecute" and devotes a line to "an unnamed indentured English servant," who prefigures in his anonymity the workers who will become afflicted with silicosis in this same country two hundred and fifty years later.[14]

Further shadowing the scene is the figure of John Brown, who occupies a central place in *The Book of the Dead*. Brown is a central figure in Rukeyser's apprehension of West Virginia as "war-born" insofar as it is

> the granite SITE OF THE precursor EXECUTION
> sabres, apostles OF JOHN BROWN LEADER OF THE
> War's brilliant cloudy RAID AT HARPERS FERRY. (72)

By interpolating her own words with those on a marker commemorating his death, Rukeyser manages to present both an "official," skeletal version of the story of John Brown and her own more nuanced version.[15] Like "the Indian Perecute, / and an unnamed indentured English servant," Brown is a "precursor," although he would seem to be precursive in a more complicated way: in the raid that he led he anticipated the Civil War, while in his execution by the state he anticipated the martyrs who were to follow in American history, most notably, in Rukeyser's generation, Sacco and Vanzetti. But Brown is also a precursor of the emancipatory power that will contest the power of Union Carbide and its hirelings, a possibility realized when a resurrected Brown returns late in *The Book of the Dead* in a utopian image: "dead John Brown's body walking from a tunnel / to break the armored and concluded mind" (102).

At the end of "West Virginia," Rukeyser shifts from the social and historical to the topographical and geological, and from a roughly documentary mode using a relatively long line to a more lyrical mode using a short, fast-moving line:

> But it was always the water
> the power flying deep

14. In histories of the expedition other than that in Conley's *West Virginia*, the indentured servant is named as Jack Weeson or Neeson.

15. Rukeyser apparently simplified the wording on a historical marker erected in 1932 in Charles Town, West Virginia. The marker reads: "JOHN BROWN SCAFFOLD / WITHIN THESE GROUNDS A SHORT DISTANCE EAST OF THIS MARKER IS THE SITE OF THE SCAFFOLD ON WHICH JOHN BROWN, LEADER OF THE HARPERS FERRY RAID, WAS EXECUTED DECEMBER THE SECOND, 1859." Thanks to those who provided me with information on the John Brown memorial: Patricia Chickering, Mike Jenkins, and Bruce Noble Jr. of the Harpers Ferry National Historical Park, and Dave Hubler.

green rivers cut the rock
rapids boiled down,
a scene of power.   (73)

In this shift to natural features, Rukeyser does not abandon her concern
with the human: her focus on "power" carries through her meditations on
both the historical and the natural dimensions.

Here the power of nature becomes uncertainly linked with human
power, which is appropriate since the longer poem presents human power
in a richly, yet painfully, ambivalent manner. This natural power is avail-
able for humanity to tap into, but tapping it is dangerous and potentially
destructive. Lest such a concern appear to be an emptily abstract truth,
Rukeyser breaks the thought of the poem's speaker at this point:

Done by the dead.
Discovery learned it.
And the living? (73)

The European discovery of the country that was to become West Virginia,
the American Revolution, the Civil War, and the making of the tunnel were
all "done by the dead." And from here Rukeyser opens the poem out onto
the vista of present-day Gauley Bridge and its environs in the wake of the
construction of the tunnel. The "West Virginia" section thus moves between
the objective facts of topography and a history of exploration and conflict,
and the subjectivity of the poetic consciousness meditating upon the mean-
ing of these facts.

Facts are overwhelmingly the focus of the third poem, "Statement:
Philippa Allen," which represents *The Book of the Dead* at its documentary
extreme: it is drawn entirely from the transcript of a hearing before a sub-
committee of the Committee on Labor, House of Representatives, Seventy-
Fourth Congress. Chaired by Glenn Griswold (D-Ind.), the subcommittee
included Jennings Randolph (D-W.Va.), Matthew A. Dunn (D-Pa.), W. P.
Lambertson (R-Kan.), and Vito Marcantonio (R-N.Y.), the last of whom
Martin Cherniack credits with providing the subcommittee with "moral
and intellectual guidance."[16] Ostensibly organized to investigate "condi-
tions of workers employed in the construction and maintenance of public
utilities" (this phrase provided the title of the transcript of the hearing),
the subcommittee actually concentrated on the Gauley Tunnel tragedy. The
investigation produced some two hundred pages of testimony and culmi-
nated in a report finding Union Carbide at fault in the disaster. As noted,

16. Cherniack, *Hawk's Nest Incident*, 75.

however, the subcommittee was denied both the funding and the power of subpoena necessary to conduct a more far-reaching and conclusive investigation.

As in the other documentary poems, testimony before the subcommittee provides Rukeyser's major—indeed, in this case, her only—resource. Rukeyser moves around freely in Allen's testimony and reorders it so as to begin with a statement establishing Allen's acquaintance with the Gauley Tunnel disaster:

> —You like the State of West Virginia very much, do you not?
> —I do very much, in the summertime.
> —How much time have you spent in West Virginia?
> —During the summer of 1934, when I was doing social work down there,
> I first heard of what we were pleased to call the Gauley tunnel tragedy,
> which involved about 2,000 men.   (73)

After establishing the authority of the speaker, Rukeyser moves to the central task of the poem, which is to establish the basic physical dimensions involved and the conditions that prevailed in the construction of the tunnel:

> According to estimates of contractors
> 2,000 men were
>   employed there
>   period, about 2 years
>   drilling, 3.75 miles of tunnel.
> To divert water (from New River)
> to a hydroelectric plant (at Gauley Junction).
> The rock through which they were boring was of a high silica content.
> In tunnel No. 1 it ran 97–99% pure silica.
> The contractors
>   knowing pure silica
>   30 years' experience
>   must have known danger for every man
> neglected to provide the workmen with any safety device. . . . (73–74)

Rukeyser makes Allen's the first voice to speak of the disaster, in homage to Allen's efforts at uncovering and publicizing it. In a note appended to the first edition of *U.S. 1*, Rukeyser indicated her debt to "the work of many investigators and writers, notably Philippa Allen."[17]

Furthermore, by having Allen speak first and most fully about these conditions, Rukeyser reflects, with documentary accuracy, the place Allen occupies in the transcript of the subcommittee's hearings, where much of the later testimony illustrates Allen's initial statement. At the hearing, Allen

17. Muriel Rukeyser, *U.S. 1*, 147.

was allowed to speak without interruption for considerable stretches of time, but by excerpting and arranging the passages as she does, Rukeyser reworks Allen's testimony into a dramatic question-and-answer format with a staccato rhythm occasionally broken by several lines of commentary or reminiscence by Allen. As M. L. Rosenthal notes: "Though the technique may seem 'unpoetic,' it is a logical result of much modern experimentation with colloquial rhythms, as well as of the contemporary interest in documentary materials."[18] Rosenthal's point is a good one: the technique is "unpoetic" by the standards of a purely lyrical or a purely organic conception of poetry, but is quite consistent with Pound's use of documents in *The Cantos* (a point made by William Carlos Williams in his review of *U.S. 1*)[19] and, less obviously, with the kind of poetry based on the contemporary American speaking voice that Robert Frost pioneered in *North of Boston*.

The emphasis on fact is continued tonally by the next poem in the sequence, "Gauley Bridge," in that its twelve stanzas present a town characterized primarily by tedium: it is an unromantic picture of a rural small town. Rukeyser's use of closed stanzas heightens this effect; rather than providing a sense of logical completeness, in this case the closed stanzas generate a sense of enclosedness, claustrophobia. This combines with the occasionally bleak diction ("empty," "deserted," "pale," "harsh") to present an unpleasant, though not dramatically so, sense of the town that was the scene of the tragedy.

By beginning this poem "Camera at the crossing sees the city" (75), Rukeyser calls to mind the photographer of the tenth stanza of "The Road." The line also calls to mind the presence of an observing self, assembling the poem. But the references to the camera and the "camera eye" have a curious effect in the context of 1930s social documentary. The camera was typically valued for its ostensible passivity and hence neutrality in depicting reality,[20] but Rukeyser's references to it draw attention, gratuitously, as it were, to the fact that the reader is experiencing a poem about Gauley Bridge, West Virginia, not the town itself. Lyrical insofar as it conveys a distinct state of mind, but with affinities to the documentary tendency in *The Book of the Dead* insofar as it is disciplined by the concreteness and definition

---

18. M. L. Rosenthal, "Chief Poets of the American Depression: Contributions of Kenneth Fearing, Horace Gregory, and Muriel Rukeyser to Contemporary American Poetry," 470. As Michael E. Staub demonstrates in *Voices of Persuasion: Politics of Representation in 1930s America*, the urge toward documentary and attention to the speaking voice were combined in a significant body of work in the 1930s.

19. William Carlos Williams, review of *U.S. 1*, 141.

20. As Stott puts it: "The camera is a prime symbol of the thirties' mind . . . because the mind aspired to the quality of authenticity, of direct and immediate experience, that the camera captures in all its photographs" (*Documentary Expression*, 77).

of its object, by the task of presentation, the poem is located both within the poet—the "camera eye"—and out there in extended space. Again, the poem is an exploration of meanings, meanings grounded in the objective world but realized only within human subjectivity.

Rukeyser achieves this effect in part by fragmenting the point of view in the poem. The fourth line introduces "the deserted Negro standing on the corner" (75), in whose place we appear to stand briefly in the ninth stanza:

> the eyes of the Negro, looking down the track,
> hotel-man and hotel, cafeteria, camera.   (76)

Immediately following this, Rukeyser further fragments the point of view:

> And in the beerplace on the other sidewalk
> always one's harsh night eyes over the beerglass
> follow the waitress and the yellow apron.   (76)

Rukeyser exploits the grammatical ambiguity of "one's" so that it refers simultaneously to "an unnamed other's," "your," and "my," locating the reader firmly within a scene presented as unceremoniously, unremarkably plain. "Gauley Bridge" thus has elements of both the lyrical and the epic/documentary about it: the subjectivity of the speaking voice inclines it toward the lyrical, while the fragmentation of that subjectivity offers the possibility of a kind of objectivity, a possibility underscored by the final lines of the poem, in which Rukeyser, directly addressing the reader, defends the place in her poem of the plainness of Gauley Bridge, which becomes a kind of analogue to *The Book of the Dead*'s often prosaic, documentary language:

> What do you want—a cliff over a city?
> A foreland, sloped to sea and overgrown with roses?
> These people live here.   (76)

Rukeyser's rebuke in these lines is made all the more telling by the use of the double spondee with a single unstressed syllable, transforming an observation into an imperative.

Louise Kertesz comments: "This stanza seems addressed to those poets like MacLeish who could still write in 1933 of their nostalgia for red roofs and olive trees. Rukeyser seeks the possibility in human life where modern people must actually live it; she has no pastoral fantasies, no nostalgia for a more 'lovely' world."[21] The sheer plainness of Gauley Bridge and the

---

21. Louise Kertesz, *The Poetic Vision of Muriel Rukeyser*, 101.

poem about it elucidates Rukeyser's statement (quoted in full in the previous chapter) concerning the propriety of unpleasant and "low" matter in poetry: "[I]t is on material of this sort that poetry must now build itself, as well as on those personal responses which have always been the basis for poetry." Unlike the young MacLeish, and an entire tradition of American literature, Rukeyser will not bemoan the fate that made modern America the material basis of her poetry.

The first four poems of *The Book of the Dead*, while they may be analyzed in terms of genre, seem most significant in terms of the functions they serve in the larger poem. These poems bear the burden of providing the introductory information necessary for the reader of *The Book of the Dead*, while also introducing the formal procedures of the poem. Thus we have in these poems a short course on the history of West Virginia, a sketch of the Gauley Bridge area, and a quick résumé of the most vital information about the Gauley Tunnel tragedy, alongside lyrical reflections on the act of exploring this land and this tragedy.

Lyrical Monologues

While the first group of poems examined in this study was read sequentially, the second (as well as the third and the fourth) are organized conceptually, by genre or mode. The monologues form the major cluster of lyrical poems in *The Book of the Dead*. As noted in the previous chapter, Rukeyser's monologues tend decidedly toward the lyrical, as opposed to the dramatic pole of the form.[22] Though Rukeyser's poetic speakers are firmly located in time, place, and situation—as they could hardly help but be, since they are typically actual individuals[23]—almost none of them perform the act necessary to a dramatic monologue of addressing themselves to an auditor present within the frame of the poem. (Furthermore, one of

22. According to Alan Sinfield's preferred definition of the form, Rukeyser's monologues would qualify as dramatic (*Dramatic Monologue*, 8–22). However, in light of the poems' lyrical character and in order to lessen terminological confusion, I refer to these poems simply as monologues.

23. The exception—and a partial one at that—is the speaker of "Absalom," a composite of the voices of Emma and Charles Jones and Philippa Allen. Even this composite, however, is assigned a single, though unnamed, identity, that of Emma Jones. Rukeyser had considered not using the real names of the people figuring in *The Book of the Dead*. She announced her decision to use the real names in a letter to Horace Gregory: "By the way, I asked you about use of real names in the Gauley Bridge thing. I'm going to use all of them, and base the use on the testimony given to Marcantonio's Senate [*sic*] Committee. If anyone wants to get angry, the Government is my backing. And I think there's a point in using real names here" (July 27, 1937, Gregory Papers).

the poems in this group, "The Face of the Dam: Vivian Jones," is presented in the third rather than the first person.) The powerfully lyrical nature of these monologues corresponds with the most significant feature that defines these poems collectively: they are subordinate to *The Book of the Dead* as a whole. Whereas monologues such as Browning's "My Last Duchess" or Tennyson's "St. Simeon Stylites" are, in poetic terms, whole units unto themselves, the monologues of *The Book of the Dead* depend upon the surrounding long poem for their significance, even as they contribute to its construction.

The speakers or characters in these poems gain most of their significance in relation to that which is explored outside rather than inside the bounds of any particular poem. In addition to explaining the lyrical as opposed to the dramatic nature of these poems when considered as monologues, this subordinate function also explains why these monologues, unlike those studied by Robert Langbaum, require little "tension between sympathy and moral judgment" in order to be successful.[24] The tensions structuring a poem such as "My Last Duchess" are developed within the poem itself. As Langbaum argues, Browning's poem is interesting because our response to the Duke does not stop at our disapproval of his odious character: we sympathetically see things through his eyes even as we judge him on the basis of that vision. The tension operative in the monologues of *The Book of the Dead* is of a very different character, because it does not derive from any relationship between sympathy and judgment—the reader is encouraged overwhelmingly to be sympathetic, and little judgment of the speakers is called for. Rather, the tension is more formal in character, deriving from the monologues' relationship with the long poem within which they are housed. The operative poles, thus, are not sympathy and judgment but subjective and objective, individual and collective, lyrical and documentary.

The subjective pole of *The Book of the Dead*, then, is occupied by the poem's lyrical monologues. The lyric, as it has come to be understood, is oriented toward subjective experience, toward statements of feeling, and renders the internal world of the private self. Thus the monologues of *The Book of the Dead* serve as lyrical intensities amid the necessarily prosaic—though not artless—documentary sections of the poem. As a result of this function, the monologues necessarily tend toward lyrical rather than dramatic presentation: the utterances of the poetic speakers do not alter anything external to the speakers themselves (in this sense the documentary poems are more dramatic in form), but rather explore for the speakers, and even more so for the reader, the emotions generated by the individual experiences of

24. Robert Langbaum, *The Poetry of Experience: The Dramatic Monologue in Modern Literary Tradition*, 85.

a transindividual tragedy. The objective and subjective worlds disclosed in the documentary poems and the monologues are bridged in the third major type of poem found in *The Book of the Dead*, the meditative poems.

The first poem in the monologue group is actually a third-person portrait and not a first-person monologue; yet functionally, "The Face of the Dam: Vivian Jones" accomplishes an end similar to that of the monologues properly so-called. Organized according to the one-hour walk of a former locomotive operator on the hydroelectric project, it opens with the title character leaving town on his way up to Hawk's Nest, which overlooks the river and the dam, a short distance outside Gauley Bridge. The poem, which consists of Jones's reflections as occasioned by the sight of the hydroelectric complex, typifies Rukeyser's practice of multiplying the perspectives on the tragedy and on the scene of the tragedy, a practice that has been compared to that of Edgar Lee Masters by Louis Untermeyer and M. L. Rosenthal.[25]

Jones's reflections essentially constitute a continuation of the last three stanzas of "West Virginia" insofar as they are poised between a sense of the beauty, or at least the magnitude, of the project—which is closely related to the proximity the project affords to the power of the basic processes of nature—and a sense of the suffering and desolation produced by the project as it was actually realized.

> There, where the men crawl, landscaping the grounds
> at the power-plant, he saw the blasts explode
> the mouth of the tunnel that opened wider
> when precious in the rock the white glass showed. (76)

The dual nature of Jones's reflections is summarized well in these four lines, as is to a great extent the double perception that Rukeyser attempts to synthesize. For the lines describe in schematic fashion the horror of the tragedy—indeed, the tragedy's most base aspect—since "opened wider" refers to the expansion of the circumference of the tunnel to provide access to the large deposits of silica. Yet the last line of the stanza, which violates ordinary usage by displacing "the white glass showed" to the end of the line in order to preserve the rhyme scheme, simultaneously drawing the reader's attention toward the phrase, emphasizes the beauty of the natural element that was the instrument of the workers' destruction.

This two-sidedness remains utterly unsynthesized, as indicated by the back-and-forth nature of stanzas 6–8:

25. Untermeyer, "Seven Poets," 609; Rosenthal, "Chief Poets," 476.

> On the half-hour he's at Hawk's Nest over the dam,
> snow springs up as he reaches the great wall-face,
> immense and pouring power, the mist of snow,
> the fallen mist, the slope of water, glass.
>
> O the gay snow the white dropped water, down,
> all day the water rushes down its river,
> unused, has done its death-work in the country,
> proud gorge and festive water.
>
> On the last quarter he pulls his heavy collar up,
> feels in his pocket the picture of his girl,
> touches for luck—he used to as he drove
> after he left his engine; stamps in the deep snow. (76–77)

Unbearable without some kind of synthesis, the scene of this two-sided reality is abandoned as Jones "turns and stamps this off his mind again / and on the hour walks again through town" (77).

The exclusive use of closed stanzas, the relatively fixed nature of the stanzaic progression (only stanzas 2 and 3 might be considered mobile), the use of time's progress to order the poem, and the powerful closure achieved by concluding the first and the last lines of the poem with the same word ("town"), all lend "The Face of the Dam" a sense of deliberateness that, rather than indicating control or conclusiveness, suggests a kind of stasis. Jones puts himself in the vicinity of the tragedy and reflects on it, but comes to no conclusion such as that which Rukeyser pursues in *The Book of the Dead*. In essence, Rukeyser uses this poem as Alan Sinfield argues postromantic poets have typically used the monologue: to present a partial view of some matter, without the necessity of committing the whole poetic self to that particular moment.[26] Rhetorically, the poem also argues that the difficulty of reconciling the power, beauty, and brutality of the dam is not a problem for the poet only, but also for those people who "live here." Implicitly, the poem argues for the necessity of synthesis, but the task itself is left for later.

The relative detachment of "The Face of the Dam" contrasts with the immediacy of "Mearl Blankenship," whose title character is directly involved in the Gauley Tunnel tragedy. The poem consists of five sections, two of third-person description of the title character (lines 1–7, 30–36), one of direct address by Blankenship to the poetic speaker (lines 8–16), and two that form the poem's emotional core, derived from a letter by Blankenship (lines 17–29, 37–49).[27] The poem thus approximates the epistolary form of

26. Sinfield, *Dramatic Monologue*, 320, 64–66.
27. Mike Gold had developed this form of poetic rewriting; see his "Examples of Worker Correspondence." Tillie Olsen's "I Want You Women Up North to Know" also

the dramatic monologue, with exterior comment provided for contextualizing purposes. The effect is fundamentally consistent with that of the more clearly lyrical monologues, primarily because the lines derived from Blankenship's letter have the emotional unity typically associated with lyrical expression.

Like the documentary sections of *The Book of the Dead*, "Mearl Blankenship" displays Rukeyser's interest in the nature and resources of language in the hands of its nonliterary users: the letter in the poem is a near transcription of a letter actually written by Blankenship. Rukeyser restricts her revisions almost exclusively to the placement of line breaks in Blankenship's original. At the point where she divides the letter into halves separated by exterior narrative comment, she omits five words, permitting her to exploit alliteration, implicit rhythm, and a rhyme that occurs in Blankenship's letter.[28] That letter, reproduced here with the lines breaking as they do on the 8½ x 5 inch original, reads in part:

> & When the shots
> Went off the boss said if
> You are going to work Venture
> back & the boss Was
> Mr Andrews & Now he is dead
> & gone But I am still here
> a lingering along & is affected
> very bad.

Rukeyser changes this to:

> & when the shots went off the boss said
> If you are going to work Venture back
> & the boss was Mr. Andrews
> & now he is dead and gone
> But I am still here
> a lingering along   (80)

Rukeyser makes the lines into coherent phrasal units (the words spoken by Mr. Andrews thus occupy a single line, for example) and establishes a rough regularity: two four-stress lines followed by two three-stress lines, each with a pyrrhic foot, and two syllabically shorter three-stress lines.

---

transforms a nonliterary into a literary document through the application of some basic revisions.

28. The letter is preserved in the Rukeyser Papers. In addition to the revisions noted here, Rukeyser also regularized somewhat Blankenship's spelling and capitalization. Oddly, she also introduced a misspelling, "tunnell" (line 23), where Blankenship spelled the word correctly, at least as I read his handwriting.

These revisions combine to produce the stanza's strong and poignant closure.

Rukeyser here inserts narrative commentary, characterizing Blankenship from the outside:

> He stood against the rock
> facing the river
> grey river grey face
> the rock mottled behind him
> like X-ray plate enlarged
> diffuse and stony
> his face against the stone. (80)

Michael Thurston has noted astutely: "The scene is Blankenship himself writ large. The river is the color of his face, and the rock against which he stands is transformed into an enlarged X ray of his own lungs. The adjective Rukeyser uses to describe the rock, *mottled,* occurs at several points in the poem to describe a silicotic lung." Thurston goes on to describe Blankenship accurately as "a metonymy for the region itself."[29] The narrative commentary thus does what Blankenship himself could hardly do.

The poem now returns to Blankenship's letter, and like the first section derived from the letter, the second also achieves a powerful closure. The last five lines of the poem appear in the letter as

> I am a Married Man & have a
> family God knows if they can
> do anything for me it Will be
> appreciated if you can anything
> for me let me know soon

Rukeyser's version is:

> I am a Married Man and have a family. God
> knows if they can do anything for me
> it will be appreciated
> if you can do anything for me
> let me know soon   (80–81)

Rukeyser adds an omitted "do" to the penultimate line, correcting an obvious slip on Blankenship's part. She omits his closing salutation ("Yours Very Truly, / Mearl Blankenship / Gauley Bridge, W. Va. Box 422"), thus

---

29. Michael Thurston, "Documentary Modernism as Popular Front Poetics: Muriel Rukeyser's *The Book of the Dead*," 68.

permitting the grim reality of his illness to stand forth: afflicted with silicosis, the only time that can be real for him is "soon." The terse, plain expression "let me know soon" conveys more effectively than anything else might the central fact of the man's life.

In its dependence upon a document written by someone other than the poet, "Mearl Blankenship" employs a quasi-documentary procedure that literalizes the pretense of one form of monologue, the epistolary, and achieves, particularly in its final line, the intensity of emotion commonly associated with the lyric. This poem, then, can be seen as preparation for the next poem to come, "Absalom," in which Rukeyser achieves a stunning if partial synthesis of documentary procedure and lyrical effect.

As in "Mearl Blankenship," Rukeyser uses documentary material in "Absalom," as well as material derived from the Egyptian *Book of the Dead,* to produce a monologue of great emotional intensity. This poem, the most immediately emotionally effective of *The Book of the Dead,* is composed largely out of testimony delivered before the House subcommittee investigating the Gauley Tunnel tragedy. Of the poem's 78 lines, 56 are taken from testimony, while the remaining 22 are taken verbatim from or are written in close imitation of the Egyptian *Book of the Dead.* Of the 56 lines from testimony, $25\frac{1}{2}$ were originally spoken by the woman upon whom the voice in the poem is constructed, Emma Jones. Another 25 lines were originally spoken by Philippa Allen, and $5\frac{1}{2}$ were originally spoken by Emma Jones's husband, Charles Jones, himself a victim of silicosis.

A poem derived so largely from outside sources might, like many of Ezra Pound's cantos, put the reader off, in a literal sense, by opening up a distance between the words on the page, any conceivable emotion or interest motivating them, and the response of the reader to the poem. (This, of course, may be a deliberate aim of the writer: producing, for example, a "difficult" and abstruse poetry as a protest against the too-readily-available, commodified, products of mass culture.) At its least successful, the poem heavily derived from sources other than the poet's own experience may seem like little more than an academic exercise, the display of a certain type of virtuosity. Nothing could be further from the effect of "Absalom," and Rukeyser's skill in working with her material must be acknowledged. Beyond this, the poem deepens Rukeyser's exploration of discursive modes, since it achieves, on the one hand, the kind of emotional immediacy based upon the expression of a single speaker's thoughts and feelings that is characteristic of the postromantic lyric, while on the other, it is composed in large part of words spoken in a public forum, at a remove from the private interiority of the lyric.

"Absalom" is spoken by a mother, a common, working-class woman who has lost three sons, and who believes she will soon lose her husband, to silicosis. But in this poem dominated by the voice of an, in all likelihood, uneducated woman, Rukeyser draws most directly from the Egyptian *Book of the Dead*, at times quoting directly, at others slightly altering the wording, and at still others constructing new verbal formulations in the style of the *Book of the Dead*. Rukeyser, then, manages to achieve the most immediate, visceral impact in the same poem in which she weaves together most tightly the Gauley Tunnel tragedy, the mythical framework through which it is (in part, at least) presented, and the documentary sources from which she reconstructs the event.

In this poem, Rukeyser expands the mythical framework of *The Book of the Dead* to include the story of Absalom from the Second Book of Samuel, chapters 13–19, primarily calling upon the story as a lament for a dead son. In the Old Testament, Absalom, the son of David, leads a rebellion against his father. Absalom is killed by David's advisor, Joab, against David's orders, and upon hearing of the death of his son, David falls into mourning: "O my son Absalom, my son, my son Absalom! would God I had died for thee, O Absalom, my son, my son!" (2 Sam. 18:33). Rukeyser would appear also to be calling upon the implication that Absalom was justified in his rebellion against David. In the Second Book of Samuel, Absalom has his half-brother Amnon killed for the rape of his sister Tamar. David, enraged at Absalom, sends him into exile, eventually relents, and permits him to return, but refuses to speak with him. It is then that Absalom stages his rebellion. While Rukeyser does not use the bulk of the Absalom story, she does carry over the sense that the son whose death is being lamented has been wronged, and that the son is righteous. This sense of the righteousness of the deceased connects the Old Testament story with the Egyptian *Book of the Dead* in Rukeyser's poem.

The poem begins with lines taken from Philippa Allen's testimony concerning Emma Jones. In the transcript of the hearings, this reads:

> It was a Mrs. Jones who first discovered what was killing these tunnel workers. Mrs. Jones had three sons—Shirley, aged 17; Owen, aged 21; and Cecil, aged 23—who worked in the tunnel with their father. Before they went to work in the tunnel, Mr. Jones and Cecil and Owen worked in a coal mine; but it was not steady work, because the mines were not going much of the time. . . .
>
> Then one of the foremen of the New Kanawha Power Co. learned that the Joneses made home brew, and he formed a habit of dropping in evenings to drink it. It was he who persuaded the boys and their fathers [*sic*] to give up their jobs in the coal mine and take on this other work, which would pay them better. Shirley, the youngest son and his mother's favorite, went into the tunnel, too.[30]

30. House Subcommittee of the Committee on Labor, *Investigation Relating to Conditions of Workers Employed in the Construction and Maintenance of Public Utilities*, 74th Cong., 2d sess., 1936, 6.

Rukeyser renders this:

> I first discovered what was killing these men.
> I had three sons who worked with their father in the tunnel:
> Cecil, aged 23, Owen, aged 21, Shirley, aged 17.
> They used to work in a coal mine, not steady work
> for the mines were not going much of the time.
> A power Co. foreman learned that we made home brew,
> he formed a habit of dropping in evenings to drink,
> persuading the boys and my husband—
> give up their jobs and take this other work.
> It would pay them better.
> Shirley was my youngest son; the boy.
> He went into the tunnel.   (81)

Rukeyser makes Allen's language tighter, more efficient, and translates it into the mother's first person. At this point the poem relies entirely upon transcribed testimony, although this is masked by the monologue format, which omits the questions that prompted the statements Rukeyser uses.

But the next two lines, themselves quotations, disrupt any notion that this poem is of a strictly documentary character:

> *My heart my mother my heart my mother*
> *My heart my coming into being.*   (81)

These lines are taken almost directly from the E. A. Wallis Budge edition of the Egyptian *Book of the Dead:* "My heart, my mother; my heart, my mother! My heart whereby I came into being!" Rukeyser appropriates the words of the prayer and the purpose of this section of the Egyptian *Book of the Dead:* to proclaim the deceased to be one "whose word is true" and who is "holy and righteous,"[31] attributes that Rukeyser assigns also to Emma Jones's son Shirley.

Rukeyser alternates between testimony delivered in a public forum by more than one speaker, which is rendered as a lyric monologue, and quotations from a mythic text, which are incorporated into the poem, though not into the monologue itself. She continues to alternate between these elements until the conclusion of the poem, where she blurs the line between testimony, lyrical monologue, and myth:

> Shirley asked that we try to find out.
> That's how they learned what the trouble was.

31. Budge, *Egyptian Book of the Dead,* 371, 373.

> *I open out a way, they have covered my sky with crystal*
> *I come forth by day, I am born a second time,*
> *I force a way through, and I know the gate*
> *I shall journey over the earth among the living.*
>
> He shall not be diminished, never;
> I shall give a mouth to my son.   (82–83)

The desire for knowledge of the cause of the tragedy is linked to rebirth in these lines, in which, once again, Rukeyser moves from the transcript of the hearings (in the first two lines quoted above) to the Egyptian *Book of the Dead* (in the next four), using her previous procedure of italicizing quotations from or lines inspired by the Egyptian text. Walter Kalaidjian reads these lines as being spoken by the mother.[32] They would appear, however, to be the words of the dead son Shirley, who speaks them just as a dead man equipped with the Egyptian *Book of the Dead* would recite his prayers. Shirley "shall journey over the earth among the living" through his mother, who becomes the agent of both his birth and his rebirth. Finally, in the last two lines, Rukeyser dramatically merges the two texts just as she merges the son with the mother, since these two lines do not occur in any form in the testimony, while they strongly resemble (without being direct quotations) lines in the Egyptian *Book of the Dead*. Most significantly, the last line, "I shall give a mouth to my son," combines a formula typical of the Egyptian text with a description of the act of the mother in testifying before the House subcommittee.

Rukeyser employs documentary and mythological materials to create a lyrical poem. Emma Jones's words appear to be delivered into that indefinite space in which the lyric may be overheard—the voice is that of "the poet talking to himself—or to nobody," as Eliot puts it[33]—with the culminating words expressing the mother's vow to keep alive the memory of her dead son. Yet those same words seem also to describe the plain fact of what the historical Emma Jones did by speaking out about the death of her family. The redemptive value that Rukeyser finds in the mother's crusade to expose the disaster inflicted upon the tunnel workers and their families and to win compensation from the parties responsible occupies both the subjective-lyrical and the objective-documentary levels of the poem: these sundered halves of modern existence are—momentarily, at least—united.

"Absalom" might thus be seen as a poem of what Ernst Bloch calls *latency*—the not-readily-apparent unity of subject and object that prefigures the moment at which history comes under genuine human control. For

---

32. Walter Kalaidjian, *American Culture between the Wars: Revisionary Modernism and Postmodern Critique*, 173–74.
33. T. S. Eliot, *The Three Voices of Poetry*, 6.

Bloch, this latency and its counterpart, *tendency*, are fundamentally a matter not only of artistic practice, but also of artistic truth, a truth understood as "the demonstration of tendency and latency of what has not yet developed and needs its agent."[34] Because both tendency and latency are crucial elements in Rukeyser's poetics, it is worth pausing a moment to define these terms more exactly. For Bloch, as for Rukeyser, history understood as a process is neither an amorphous going forward nor a merely passive unfolding, but rather "an energetic straining, created by impending possibilities."[35] These impending possibilities straining to be realized but, to use the single formulation most characteristic of Bloch, "not yet" realized are what in the historical realm people try to realize in society, and what in the aesthetic realm artists try to realize in works of art.

Tendency thus refers to the directional movement of the process, and *latency* to the content of the process. *Latency* describes the unrealized potential of the object world, those things which are in process and which need to be brought into a more adequate relation with the subject. Fredric Jameson sees *tendency* and *latency* as "two different languages or terminological systems," with *tendency* characterized by "the movement of the world in time toward the future's ultimate moment," and *latency* by "the more spatial notion of that adequation of object to subject which must characterize that moment's content."[36] As Jameson's language makes clear, Bloch's notion of process, and his terms *tendency* and *latency,* are part of the central concern of his aesthetic and his philosophy: the utopian.

As a poem of latency, "Absalom" presents the formal union of the private, lyrical subject—the speaking voice of the poem—with the public voices of those who testified before the House subcommittee, especially that of Emma Jones. The inwardness of the lyric and the outwardness of congressional testimony meet in a symbolic, prefigurative union of these seemingly irreconcilable dimensions of modern existence, whose mutual repugnance is fixed within the generic divisions of literary study. Thus "Absalom" is an overwhelmingly powerful poem both on the sheer emotional level of a mother's story of the greed and cowardice of Union Carbide and the image of her son wasted by disease, and on the level of the formal, generic means by which Rukeyser presents this material. The fusion of emotional content and formal construction renders "Absalom" the complex climax of the lyrical monologues.

The power of "Absalom"—both its purely emotional power and its deep utopian resonance—contrasts with the relative failure of "George Robin-

34. Ernst Bloch, "Marxism and Poetry," 161.
35. Wayne Hudson, *The Marxist Philosophy of Ernst Bloch,* 114.
36. Fredric Jameson, *Marxism and Form: Twentieth-Century Dialectical Theories of Literature,* 146.

son: Blues." (Rukeyser may have gotten the name wrong: it appears in the transcript of the House testimony as George Robison.) While Rukeyser thought highly enough of "George Robinson: Blues" to include it in a later volume of her selected poetry, it is arguably the least successful individual poem in *The Book of the Dead*.[37] This is largely a function of Rukeyser's attempt to write the poem in the form of a blues lyric. Rukeyser described the poem as "a free fantasy on the blues form. . . . one of the loosest possible variations on it."[38] Despite the looseness with which she uses the form, the blues lyric imposes on her formal conventions such as end rhyme that lead her to fill out lines just as the demands of traditional versification would— one of the imperatives of traditional poetry that the early modernists objected to most forcefully. One need only think of Pound's three principles in "A Retrospect," the second of which famously enjoins poets to "use absolutely no word that does not contribute to the presentation."[39] While her poetics were certainly not identical to Pound's, Rukeyser was committed to the principle of linguistic efficiency, thus making her decision to write the poem in the blues format—padding out lines and weakening her diction in order to maintain a rhyme scheme—appear to be mistaken within the terms of her own poetics.

Two stanzas will illustrate the problem and the partial failure of Rukeyser's attempt to "extend the document" in this poem:

> Did you ever bury thirty-five men in a place in back of your house,
> thirty-five tunnel workers the doctor didn't attend,
> died in the tunnel camps, under rocks, everywhere, world without end.
>
> When a man said I feel poorly, for any reason, any weakness or such,
> letting up when he couldn't keep going barely,
> the Cap and company come and run him off the job surely.   (84)

These lines, like most of "George Robinson," are derived from Robison's testimony before the subcommittee. The section from which Rukeyser draws reads:

> **Mr. Robison.** If a colored man was sick and really couldn't go to work in the morning, he had to hide out before the shack rouster came around. That fellow had two pistols and blackjack to force the men to go to work. He was

---

37. "George Robinson: Blues" is one of six poems from *The Book of the Dead* chosen for *Waterlily Fire: Poems 1935–1962*.

38. Muriel Rukeyser, interview by Harry T. Moore et al., in Charles Madden, ed., *Talks with Authors*, 130. The interview was conducted as part of a 1964 session hosted by Stephens College in which Rukeyser participated via telephone hook-up.

39. Ezra Pound, *Literary Essays*, 3.

a fat man and we called him what we called most of the other white men around there, "Cap." . . .

When it got so a worker couldn't make it at all, when he got sick and simply couldn't go longer, the sheriff would come around and run him off the place, off the works. I have seen the sheriff and his men run the workers off their places when they were sick and weak, so sick and weak that they could hardly walk. . . .

Many of the men died in the tunnel camps; they died in hospitals, under rocks, and every place else. A man named Finch, who was known to me, died under a rock from silicosis. I can go right now and point to many graves only two blocks from where I live there now.

Mr. Griswold. How many men did you help bury—about how many?

Mr. Robison. I helped to bury about 35, I would say.[40]

Unlike Rukeyser's reworking of testimony elsewhere, or her slight alterations of Mearl Blankenship's letter, the versification of this document adds extraneous elements, rather than concentrating and emphasizing elements already present in the prose source. The phrase "world without end," for example, serves only to fill out the line and make a rhyme with "attend." Rukeyser's considerable abilities as a poet do not lend themselves best to closed form, even when such a form is vernacular.

However, her use of the blues form becomes looser in the second half of the poem, relying more upon repetition and slant rhyme than upon conventional full rhyme; as a result, these lines seem less contrived. Rukeyser also makes a major alteration in the testimony. In his statement before the House subcommittee, Robison recounted:

As dark as I am, when I came out of that tunnel in the mornings, if you had been in the tunnel too and had come out at my side, nobody could have told which was the white man. The white man was just as black as the colored man. . . .

The groves near the camps had trees that were all colored with this dust. . . . There was so much dust around those groves or parks that it looked like someone had sprinkled flour around the place. It really looked pretty. Even the rain would not wash away that dust in the parks or groves.[41]

Rukeyser reverses the order of these two sections, permitting the observation about the dust covering the tunnel workers to close the poem:

Looked like somebody sprinkled flour all over the parks and groves,
it stayed and the rain couldn't wash it away and it twinkled
that white dust really looked pretty down around our ankles.

40. House Subcommittee, *Investigation Relating to Conditions of Workers,* 67–68.
41. Ibid., 67.

As dark as I am, when I came out at morning after the tunnel at night,
with a white man, nobody could have told which man was white.
The dust had covered us both, and the dust was white.   (85)

In addition to reversing the order of Robison's statement, Rukeyser also
changes his testimony about the dust produced in the tunnel. Making the
dust with which the men were covered white instead of black renders it
consistent with its looking like flour. Rukeyser likely corrected Robison's
memory, thereby making the image in his testimony more compatible with
the image pattern developed throughout *The Book of the Dead* of the simul-
taneously beautiful, useful, and deadly silica dust.[42] Indeed, these last lines
are an important part of this emerging pattern; Rukeyser makes the dust
central at the end of this poem, where it becomes the main topic of the last
three stanzas.

This pattern culminates in the final stanza, which breaks with the form
of all previous stanzas except the first by end-stopping the penultimate
line, thus slowing the tempo and emphasizing the last line: "The dust had
covered us both, and the dust was white." Commenting on this last line,
Rukeyser said:

[I]f the last line really works, it does it by so strong an omission that I hope
you get a suggestion of the opposite—that this likeness is inner, and not outer.
I think if this sort of thing works, it works, as it does for me in the plays of
Tennessee Williams, when you get so strong a suggestion of perfect love, of
married love, of the love that is absolutely left out of the writing that the
suggestion of the opposite comes through.

The dust here thus plays a complex role; it is simultaneously literally a
pathogen ("The dust was white. The dust was fatal to most people"),[43]
something pretty, and a potential principle of unity between the white and
black workers, whose common mortality and vulnerability to exploitation

42. It is also possible that Robison's memory was not at fault, and that he merely
drew upon his memory of different episodes in the construction of the tunnel. When
they were not drilling through sandstone, the workers were at least part of the time
drilling through shale, when they may very well have been covered with dust and dirt
that was not white. David Kadlec sees Robison's inconsistency as the product both of
the politics of racial imposture, whereby whites may impersonate blacks but blacks may
not impersonate whites, and of Robison's desire to emphasize the racial character of the
Gauley Tunnel tragedy (Kadlec, "X-Ray Testimonials," 24–25).

43. Rukeyser, interview, *Talks with Authors*, 131. Rukeyser's reaction to Williams's
plays further suggests the deep similarity between her sensibility and that of Ernst
Bloch. They share a sharp awareness of the mechanism by which the positive is sug-
gested via the negative, an aesthetics of absence.

it reveals. As Rukeyser almost certainly would have known, George Robison was dead within two months of testifying before the sub-committee.[44]

Unlike "George Robinson: Blues," "Juanita Tinsley" portrays someone who was not directly a victim of the tunnel disaster but whose life and sensibility has been marked by the tragedy, one of those "untouched people [who] have been touched and changed."[45] Focused on one woman's personal response, the poem deals with the aftermath of the tragedy: Tinsley was a member of the Gauley Bridge Committee, a local defense committee organized to assist the victims of the tragedy, and the speaker is poised between two postures. First, she feels a sense of responsibility to help alleviate the suffering caused by the disaster, despite the ease with which she can be distracted into unawareness:

> I know in America there are songs,
> forgetful ballads to be sung,
> but at home I see this wrong.   (85)

Yet in the last stanza Tinsley also looks to escape the sense of desolation of which the tragedy is both part and symbol:

> The scene of hope's ahead; look, April,
> and next month with a softer wind,
> maybe they'll rest upon their land,
> and then maybe the happy song, and love,
> a tall boy who was never in a tunnel.   (86)

While M. L. Rosenthal takes these lines (and Tinsley's reported absence from the meeting in the poem "Praise of the Committee") to indicate that her petit bourgeois sympathy with the workers is not fundamentally serious, this seems an unnecessarily severe reading. In the outline Rukeyser used in her attempt to make a film about the Gauley Tunnel tragedy, she refers to Juanita Tinsley as "the brightest girl in the high-school. She is fifteen, with a pale-glowing, luminous face, a village Joan of Arc, once she has heard what she is to do."[46] Rukeyser does not appear to have intended to depict Tinsley negatively, as Rosenthal would have it.

44. Philippa Allen, "Gauley Bridge Death Toll Grows in Village of the Living Dead," 5.
45. Muriel Rukeyser, *Gauley Bridge*, 55.
46. "Outline Story for *Gauley Bridge*," typescript, Rukeyser Papers, 5.

Within Tinsley's desire to escape the burden that the tragedy has placed upon her and upon all those who do not turn their backs upon the disaster, Rukeyser generates a utopian symbol of relief from the destruction that surrounds her: "A tall boy who was never in a tunnel." This modest image represents the individual fulfillment of love—the topic of so many of those "forgetful ballads"—for Tinsley, which seems quite apart from if not (à la Rosenthal) contradictory to the engagement in a collective search for justice in which she is engaged. Yet "a tall boy who was never in a tunnel" also stands as a symbol of a humanity freed of the burden borne by those who died, and thus free to walk with the "upright gait" that for Bloch represents a humanity in full possession of its dignity, freed of "the distortions and disfigurements which an alienating society based on the division of labor has inflicted."[47] The entire logic of *The Book of the Dead* should lead us to see this desire for "a tall boy" as an individual correlate of, rather than the opposite of, the struggle waged by Tinsley as a member of the Gauley Bridge Committee.

While "Juanita Tinsley" presents the coherent, if private, reflections of someone not directly affected by the Gauley Tunnel tragedy, "Arthur Peyton" is severely fragmented and spoken by someone whose life has been blighted. The fragmentation of the poem emerges from the crosscutting among the speaker's private reflections, lines addressed to his beloved, and lines drawn from testimony. Through this fragmentation Rukeyser attempts to convey the pain of a man who has been wronged, whose life has been cut severely short, and for whom love means pain, knowing as he does that his love stands under a sentence of death. The speaker is an engineer who was employed by Union Carbide's subsidiary, the New Kanawha Power Company, and whose exposure to silica dust led to silicosis severe enough that he was given only two years to live by his doctor when it was first detected. Peyton testified before the House subcommittee, and roughly 15 of the poem's 43 lines are derived from this testimony.

Apparently Peyton is the "one" whose "harsh night eyes over the beerglass / follow the waitress and the yellow apron" (76) in "Gauley Bridge," since in the present poem he watches his love wait on tables across the street.[48] The poem's first stanza registers Peyton's feelings about his fate, immediately followed by an excerpt from a letter he received from the attorneys who settled out of court (under terms very favorable to themselves) a lawsuit filed against Rinehart and Dennis and the New Kanawha Power Company. In this way, Rukeyser introduces the three major threads that run

47. Zipes, "Toward a Realization of Anticipatory Illumination," xxvii; Ernst Bloch, *The Principle of Hope*, 2:453.
48. In the filmscript *Gauley Bridge*, Peyton is in love with Frances Jones, daughter of Emma and Charles Jones.

through the poem: Peyton's sense of physical obliteration, the pain caused by his doomed love, and his justified bitterness against his employers.

> Consumed. Eaten away. And love across the street.
> I had a letter in the mail this morning
> Dear Sir, . . . pleasure . . . enclosing herewith our check . . .
> payable to you, for $21.59
>   being one-half of the residue which
>   we were able to collect in your behalf
>   in regard to the above case.
> In winding up the various suits,
>   after collecting all we could,
>   we find this balance due you.
> With regards, we are
>   Very truly,   (90–91)

The letter quoted could only have deepened Peyton's bitterness, since the check for $21.59 represented his portion of the settlement agreed to by the attorneys representing him and some two hundred other workers. Of the meager settlement, the workers received only half since the attorneys were hired on the basis of a 50 percent split of any award to the plaintiffs.[49]

The three threads we see in the first stanza appear again in the second stanza, within three lines:

> O love consumed eaten away the foreman laughed
> they wet the drills when the inspectors came
> the moon blows glassy over our native river.   (91)

Here, the compression of the different elements at work in the poem is increased. The last line connects "the moon," that traditional symbol of romance, with the "river," source of the power that is channeled by the tunnel, out of which, in turn, the silica (glass) was extracted. Thus the line conveys a sense of the destruction of love and beauty by a fate written ultimately in the terms of the contract between Union Carbide and Rinehart and Dennis. It also conveys the inextricability for the speaker of love and death, beauty and pain.

---

49. Cherniack, *Hawk's Nest Incident*, 65–66. Cherniack notes evenhandedly both that the settlement was very favorable to the law firm, though not to the plaintiffs, and that the plaintiffs' case would have been extremely difficult to make in court, primarily because Union Carbide was prepared to make any action against it expensive and exhausting. Indeed, Cherniack's entire consideration of the attempt to win compensation for the tunnel workers through the legal system, under the then-existing laws, emphasizes the difficulty of such a proceeding, while not overlooking the culpability of some of the attorneys engaged to represent the workers.

"Arthur Peyton" might be seen as the opposite in *The Book of the Dead* of "Absalom" and "Juanita Tinsley," since there is little suggestion of redemption, through either love or struggle, in the poem. Rather, Peyton contemplates his transformation from animate to inanimate matter as a more or less pure experience, and the sense of doom that clouds his life and his love dominates the poem, despite the suggestion of a kind of immortality in the final stanza:

> Between us, love
> the buses at the door
> the long glass street   two years, my death to yours
> my death upon your lips
> my face becoming glass
> strong challenged time making me win immortal
> the love a mirror of our valley
> our street   our river   a deadly glass to hold.
> Now they are feeding me into a steel mill furnace
> O love the stream of glass a stream of living fire. (91)

In these lines Rukeyser exploits most fully one of the motifs she has been developing throughout the poem: glass. Made from silica, glass appears in a variety of forms in *The Book of the Dead*: the lens of the camera that takes in and frames the scene, the windows of the town's main street, the individual particles that fill the lungs of the tunnel workers, the glasslike appearance of water, the "mirror" that the doomed valley provides to Peyton's love, the heaps of extracted silica stockpiled at Alloy. Here several of these combine eerily into the image of Peyton translated into silica: "my face becoming glass," "the stream of glass a stream of living fire," as the silica is used at the steel mill in Alloy. These lines suggest the brittleness and inorganic quality of glass, as well as the infernal conditions of the blast furnace, both suggestions contrasting sharply with the tenderness of love, even as this tenderness combines with the inorganic in the image of "my face becoming glass"—in the form of a photograph of one now dead, framed and pressed behind its protective glass cover.

The negativity produced by the sense of doom with which Peyton regards love carries over into the suggestion of a kind of immortality. Even the line "strong challenged time making me win immortal," the only line in this final stanza that conveys any potentially positive content, must thus be read as ambivalent. "Strong challenged time" appears to refer to the two years Peyton has left to him, while "win" appears to be used in the sense of "earn" or possibly in light of its Old English root, *winnan*, "to strive." Yet "Arthur Peyton" does not yield the powerful sense that its speaker will live on in the way of the son in "Absalom," but rather something much more emotionally unstable. The poem is shot through with a pain conveyed through strong and complex visual imagery: "Now they are feeding me into a steel mill furnace / O love the stream of glass a stream of living fire." The final line presents a kinetic image, "a stream of living fire," that contrasts with the image of "my face becoming glass," which is static, despite the use of the participial form. The kinetic image of "a stream of living fire" resonates with "strong challenged time making me win immortal," and yet this stream does not appear redemptive in any way.

"Arthur Peyton," the fourteenth of the twenty poems of *The Book of the Dead*, the last of the monologues, and the last poem before the major contemplative sequence of "Alloy," "Power," and "The Dam," is perhaps the most ambivalent poem in the sequence. Yet somehow, despite this ambivalence, by presenting in touchingly personal terms the unredeemed harm done to a victim of Union Carbide's quest for profit, "Arthur Peyton" is also perhaps the darkest poem of *The Book of the Dead*. It may not be a gross exaggeration to say that the remainder of *The Book of the Dead* is devoted largely to "processing" the "blank," the negativity generated in "Arthur Peyton" at the level of personal experience and at the level of the collective in "Power."

Toward the end of *The Poetry of Experience*, Robert Langbaum discusses the emergence of the dramatic monologue as part of "the victory of character over action that distinguishes the high literature of modern times," as opposed to both the classical tradition's insistence on action (memorably stated in Aristotle's *Poetics*) and the mass audience's taste for action, to which character is subordinate. We might also see this victory as part of the slow emergence within capitalist modernity of the alienated individual, of which the speaking subject of the modern lyric is a prime instance. While Langbaum does not explore this, the possibility of doing so is implicit in his book. As he notes, one of the key enabling features of modern literature is the severing of the classical link between moral standards and social rank, whereby the moral behavior demanded of a king, say, differs in kind from that demanded of a woman: "The de-objectification of morality in the modern era is intimately associated with the de-objectification of rank, and both have had the same democratizing effect on literature as on society."[50] This shift also is linked to the emergence of the modern individual, since within modernity one comes to understand oneself primarily *as* an individual, and not as the occupant of a largely preordained social rank.

As a practice emergent within capitalist modernity, the modern lyric may be taken to represent the formal realization of the subject of capitalist modernity, the alienated individual. Yet at the same time the modern

50. Langbaum, *Poetry of Experience*, 210, 216. Langbaum refers to such statements of Aristotle as: "There is a manly character of bravery and fierceness which cannot, with propriety, be given to a woman" (*The Poetics of Aristotle*, 30).

lyric and the individual subject for whom it is the preeminent literary form contain within them a utopian significance in that they represent a realm of full and authentic experience not typically available to people, whether because of the exploitative and oppressive features of societies that frustrate the development of individual capacities or because of the stifling nature of the social conventions that function in such societies. Thus, for example, the figure of the romantic poet not only embodies the historical type of the entrepreneur, but also stands as a rebuke to the bloodlessness of nineteenth-century capitalist society, especially as it is seen in the figure of "the bourgeois": it is the figure of a full human existence, in which one's capacities are fully developed.

Rukeyser seems to have understood this complex relationship between poetry's capacity for truth and liability to ideology exceptionally well. *The Book of the Dead* is not a poem exclusively of the individual lyric voice, of an epic objectivity, nor of dramatic antagonism. Rather, it uses all of these modes, permitting their partial truths to emerge and form a greater—and truer—whole. Indeed, Rukeyser appears to have been especially attuned to the competing demands and historical necessity of the collective and the individual. In her biography of the American theoretical physicist Willard Gibbs, she declares her intention:

> To look for the sources of energy, sources that will enable us to find the strength for the leaps that must be made. To find sources, in our own people, in the living people. And to be able to trace the gifts made to us to two roots: the infinite anonymous bodies of the dead, and the unique few who, out of great wealth of spirit, were able to make their own gifts.[51]

If Willard Gibbs is an example of "the unique few," then surely *The Book of the Dead* is dedicated to conferring upon "the infinite anonymous bodies of the dead" the full dignity befitting their humanity and their sacrifice.

Accordingly, the monologues of *The Book of the Dead*, like many of the poems of Robert Frost, give lyric speech to social subjects typically excluded from any substantial participation in the realm of the poetic. As Frank Lentricchia points out in his discussion of Frost's sonnet "Mowing," even romantics such as Wordsworth typically present their "solitary reapers" as observed objects rather than as speaking subjects.[52] By employing a lyrical form in the monologues of *The Book of the Dead*, then, Rukeyser preserves what might be seen as one of the great, if ambivalent, gains of the capitalist era, the emergence of the modern individual, and recognizes the individuality of figures who occupy unexalted, if not despised, positions in

---

51. Rukeyser, *Willard Gibbs*, 12.
52. Frank Lentricchia, *Modernist Quartet*, 96–97.

society. That Rukeyser's practice is indeed of this character would appear to be confirmed by her correspondence with one B. W. Barnett, a former resident of Gauley Bridge, who regretted that "most of those [people] you referred to as having talked to, do not have too good a reputation in many respects." Barnett differentiated these unnamed others from Arthur Peyton, the engineer, whose family were "good people" and presumably more suitable lyric subjects, as well as more reliable witnesses.[53]

Simultaneously, by placing the dramatic monologues within the governing structure of *The Book of the Dead*, Rukeyser avoids one of the pernicious effects of the "de-objectification of rank": the reduction of society to the level of sheer artifice or unreality. Rukeyser's documentary, or social, poems do not negate her lyric, subjective poems, and vice versa. Rather, these different poetic modes reveal at the level of form different, interdependent, aspects of human reality.

53. Barnett to Rukeyser, October 20, 1943, Rukeyser Papers.

3

The Documentary Poems

"If the traditional nominalist error has been to elide
the signified, the customary post-modernist stance
has been to elide the referent."

Roy Bhaskar, *Dialectic: The Pulse of Freedom*

The documentary is the most untraditional poetic mode employed by
Rukeyser in *The Book of the Dead*, in those poems composed on the basis
of a prior written document—most notably the transcript of testimony de-
livered before the House subcommittee investigating the Gauley Tunnel
disaster. The documentary procedure in *The Book of the Dead* derives from
many sources. The 1930s were, as a number of scholars have demonstrated,
a decade in which the documentary form became extraordinarily powerful.
On the Left, "reportage" was considered a major literary form. Simultane-
ously Ezra Pound showed that it was possible to overcome the limitations
of lyric poetry through the use of nonpoetic documents within poetic texts.
A wide variety of cultural developments that led to a fascination with doc-
umentary form, and the motivations underlying these developments, are
to some degree registered by *The Book of the Dead*.

As William Stott argues in his seminal *Documentary Expression and Thir-
ties America*, the 1930s were virtually dominated by the documentary mode
of communication, in part because the seeming directness and factualness
of the documentary suited it both to the traditional American "cult of expe-
rience" (in the phrase of Philip Rahv) and to the more particular skepticism
regarding the abstract and impalpable that was engendered in the public
by the Great Depression. Documentary in the 1930s, Stott notes, was typi-
cally "social documentary," which

    deals with facts that are alterable. It has an intellectual dimension to make
    clear what the facts are, why they came about, and how they can be changed

for the better. Its more important dimension, however, is usually the emotional: feeling the fact may move the audience to wish to change it.[1]

The Book of the Dead is clearly a part of the 1930s documentary movement and, while hardly encompassed by Stott's criteria for the social documentary, certainly fits his description.

Closely related to the documentaries analyzed by Stott is the journalistic practice of reportage. Reportage as a technique of the Left was pioneered by John Reed and exemplified in highly influential form in his 1919 account of Russia's October Revolution, *Ten Days That Shook the World*. By the 1930s reportage was a standard leftist journalistic mode, and the flagship anthology *Proletarian Literature in the United States* (1935), edited by the leading literary figures of the Communist party, featured fifty pages of reportage. The editors claimed that reportage was a literary form specially characteristic of the twentieth century, and one that "assumes greater importance as the tempo of this age increases."

> [Reportage] helps the reader *experience* the event recorded. Reportage is three-dimensional reporting. The writer not only condenses reality, he must get his reader to see and feel the facts. The best writers of reportage do their editorializing via their artistry.[2]

Like the "documentary expression" studied by Stott (who considers briefly such journalists as James Rorty and John L. Spivak), reportage was a "literature of fact" that responded to the demands placed on readers and writers by the realities not only of the Depression, but also more generally of the extended period of turmoil from 1914 to 1945.

In the face of such titanic realities, imaginative literature could seem weak indeed. Whether or not one agrees with the position he takes, Ernest Hemingway states this feeling well:

> The greatest novels are made up. Everything in them is created by the author. . . . But there are events which are so great that if a writer has participated in them his obligation is to try to write them truly rather than assume the presumption of altering them with intention.[3]

A great event may overwhelm the resources of literature and the capacity of the literary writer; if one has firsthand knowledge of such an event, fidelity to the facts, according to Hemingway, is the appropriate stance for the writer.

1. Stott, *Documentary Expression*, 73, 26.
2. Granville Hicks et al., eds., *Proletarian Literature in the United States*, 211.
3. Ernest Hemingway quoted in Peter Monteath, "The Spanish Civil War and the Aesthetics of Reportage," 75.

The journalistic modes of documentary expression were typically, though not exclusively, employed by writers of leftist or Left-liberal persuasion. Paula Rabinowitz's observation about reportage could be expanded to the other closely related documentary forms:

> As a form that sought to overcome the divisions between literature and history, private thought and public action, subjectivity and objectivity, reportage appeared to overcome the contradictions literary radicals felt between their position as intellectuals and their allegiance to the working class.[4]

For leftist writers, reportage seemed to offer a solution to problems both formal and political.

In the 1930s and into the 1940s, Rukeyser was surrounded by and actively involved with the world of New Deal and leftist documentary and reportage. Indeed, she conceived of *The Book of the Dead* as, among other things, one part of a multimedia assault on the issue of silicosis. Thus, she wrote a "radio oratorio" and a screenplay for a never-to-be-produced film on the tragedy, in addition to an apparently abortive photo-essay that she intended to create in collaboration with Nancy Naumburg.[5] Rukeyser's surviving correspondence from the late 1930s reveals that she made a serious attempt to have the film produced. Among her published writings, her comments collected in *The Life of Poetry* and her two photo-essays published in *Coronet* magazine—which used the photos of the New Deal's Resettlement Administration photographers Ben Shahn, Dorothea Lange, and Arthur Rothstein—demonstrate that she shared the interest in documentary common on the Left in the 1930s.

Yet the documentary trend found its first great *poetic* exemplar in Ezra Pound, eventual adherent of Italian fascism. Pound's *Cantos,* Michael André Bernstein argues, may be understood as an attempt to undo one of the major effects of nineteenth-century French poetics (an effect paralleled less reputably and less brilliantly in the poetics of the American Genteel Tradition), particularly as seen in Mallarmé: the sundering of poetic language from the things and events of this world. Mallarmé wanted poetic language to confront a realm to which ordinary language had no access, where it was rendered silent. Pound, conversely, sought to reattach poetic language to the worldly concerns of men (as he would have put it). In his

---

4. Paula Rabinowitz, *They Must Be Represented: The Politics of Documentary*, 44.

5. Naumburg was quite active in leftist documentary filmmaking circles. She was photographer on the enacted-documentary film "Sheriffed," about which she said: "The purpose of the film is to show working-class audiences what the actual conditions in the life of the American farmer are, and the necessity for militant organization" (quoted in Ed Kennedy, "Three Workers Films," 11). The film was made on a shoestring and used farmers as actors.

attempt to achieve this, Pound incorporated extraliterary texts to serve as direct, if fragmentary, representatives of the real social and historical world from which they emerged.[6]

By the time Rukeyser began work on *The Book of the Dead*, Pound had published his first forty-one cantos in book form, and in them one finds (to give a brief but representative list) correspondence of Sigismundo Malatesta, a fifteenth-century Italian mercenary; excerpts from papal denunciations of Malatesta; correspondence between John Adams and Thomas Jefferson; speeches of Martin Van Buren; and excerpts from *The Autobiography of Lincoln Steffens*. While a direct influence of Pound on Rukeyser is not as yet provable, Rukeyser's method of composition in *The Book of the Dead*, particularly her use of documentary materials, derives from developments whose pioneer is Pound. Like leftist documentary, Pound's project also attempted to reunite culture, social reality, and political significance, though it was practiced within a very different literary culture and aimed at different political ends.[7] Formally, though not politically, Rukeyser's documentary poems have a foot in each camp, employing the deliberate fragmentation and necessary difficulty of the Poundian documentary technique in order to confront material more typical of the proletarian novel, toward ends consonant not with Pound's fascism, but with political leftism.

While part of the impetus moving Pound to develop a documentary method for modern poetry was the (negative) example of Mallarmé, the broader context was that of a reaction against the extreme subjectiveness characteristic of romanticism and powerfully expressed in the romantic lyric. As M. H. Abrams (*The Mirror and the Lamp*), Alastair Fowler (*Kinds*

6. Michael André Bernstein, *The Tale of the Tribe: Ezra Pound and the Modern Verse Epic*, 5–8. There is an interesting and informative parallel between Pound's insistence on reading original primary texts (to the extent of incorporating them in his poems) and the "new use," cited by Stott, "of 'primary sources' in college history courses" in the 1930s (*Documentary Expression*, 131).

7. While Pound's right-wing credentials are beyond question, it is worth noting that he was, as Tim Redman points out, ideologically ambidextrous enough to publish in *New Masses* as late as 1928 (*Ezra Pound and Italian Fascism*, 73–74). In any case, Rukeyser, whether or not she consciously modeled the documentary sections of *The Book of the Dead* on those of *The Cantos*, was aware of Pound. In addition to the fact that Pound pioneered the formal experimentation that Rukeyser developed further, it is clear from Rukeyser's papers that she read Pound. She typed out the reading list from Pound's *How to Read* sometime in the late 1930s (the list is undated; Rukeyser Papers). In addition, her friendships with H.D. and, probably more significantly, Hugh MacDiarmid put her in touch with poets (in MacDiarmid's case, an explicitly Marxist poet) for whom Pound was a vital presence. Finally, Rukeyser drew a map of the Gauley Bridge area and signed it "MR fecit," suggestive of the line from Canto 45, "Adamo me fecit" (Adam made me). When William Carlos Williams commented that Rukeyser wrote portions of her documentary poems "with something of the skill employed by Pound in the material of his 'Cantos,'" he registered a fundamental formal similarity between Pound and Rukeyser (review of *U.S. 1*, 141).

of Literature), David Lindley (*Lyric*), and others have shown, the lyric underwent a decisive transformation in the early years of romanticism, as part of the history of a continuous transformation of the form: it became interiorized. The pivotal feature of the lyric became its quality of expressing the interior thoughts and feelings of the poetic speaker. Running parallel to this interiorization of the lyric is the historical development of the model of the artist as an alienated, though not necessarily oppositional, figure at odds with the prevailing standards—cultural, social, and/or political—of the day. Lindley puts the matter succinctly: the interiorization of the lyric bears "witness to the poets' growing sense of alienation from the urban, materialist world and the retreat to the solitary world of the mind; to the erosion of stable religious, social, and political belief; to the profound alteration in the range and scope of poetry's world effected by the growth of the novel and so on."[8] Thus both the mode of expression and the self-understanding of the romantic and postromantic poet tended toward subjectivity and isolation from social reality.

It is in this sense that the lyric came to be understood as the characteristic discourse of the isolate subject. As Theodor Adorno puts it:

> The subjective being that makes itself heard in lyric poetry is one which defines and expresses itself as something opposed to the collective and the realm of objectivity. While its expressive gesture is directed toward, it is not intimately at one with nature. It has, so to speak, lost nature and seeks to recreate it through personification and through descent into the subjective being itself.[9]

Not only is modern lyric expression necessarily distant from the objective world in the form of nature, it is also distant from the objective world in the form of society, which, unlike nature, is typically understood to be that which the lyric excludes—indeed, as that which *must be* excluded as a necessary condition of lyric expression as such. Adorno argues that despite this apparently asocial character of lyric expression, objective social content remains within it, though transformed by and enfolded within individual consciousness.

The objective social content that Adorno finds latent within all lyric poetry does not, in *The Book of the Dead*, remain latent. Rukeyser does not permit objective content to remain merely implicit in the lyric; she renders it explicit in the documentary sections of the poem, which, as we have seen, are often edited and slightly revised versions of testimony offered before the House subcommittee investigating the construction of the tunnel at Gauley Mountain. These documentary sections are oriented toward the

8. David Lindley, *Lyric*, 69.
9. T. W. Adorno, "Lyric Poetry and Society," 59.

objective world, toward statements of fact, and render the world of public discourse.

The documentary character of *The Book of the Dead* may be seen primarily in "Statement: Philippa Allen," "Praise of the Committee," "The Disease," "The Doctors," "The Disease: After-Effects," and "The Bill." But before we turn to the poems themselves, it should be acknowledged that, following the structuralist and poststructuralist turns in literary theory and criticism, the documentary form stands suspect, claiming as it does to provide access to reality—a reality of which our understanding is shaped by the very mode of access provided by the documentary. As Michael E. Staub points out, the documentary form has, like traditional ethnography, become the object of poststructuralist criticism for claiming to provide unproblematic, transparent access to the real.[10] Such access is impossible, poststructuralists argue, since the reality to which the documentary claims to be faithful is in fact constructed by the practice of documentary. Documentary thus does not provide access to the truth, but rather a construction of reality faithful to the perceptions, needs, and desires of the documentarian—all of which are determined by preexistent ideological and/or cultural schemas rather than by a notional objective reality.

As Brian Winston summarizes the poststructuralist objection to documentary: "A representation is a representation is a representation. The real has nothing to do with it." While Winston does not appear to embrace the poststructuralist position wholeheartedly, its force may be felt throughout his argument, leading him to say:

> The basic fact is that we can no longer look at photographs as windows on the world whose panes have been polished to a preternatural transparency by the glazier/photographer. Our sophistication now is such that we will always see the marks on the glass.[11]

While this statement indicates an unobjectionable awareness of the role of the perceiver in perception, it also indicates a quite objectionable confusion of epistemology and ontology, signifier and referent. Indeed, the last sentence, rather than indicating the superiority of "our sophistication," reveals the precise weakness of the poststructuralist position. When Winston writes "we will *always* see the marks on the glass" (my emphasis), he creates a crucial ambiguity. Will the marks on the glass, rather than something else, be what we see always? Or will our seeing that something else, that which is being represented, always be affected, though not precluded, by the marks on the glass? Between these two interpretations lies a vast gulf.

10. Staub, *Voices of Persuasion*, 3–4.
11. Brian Winston, *Claiming the Real: The Griersonian Documentary and Its Legitimations*, 244, 251–52.

The poststructuralist emphasis on the signifier and the related destruction of any pretense of access to reality is especially corrosive to documentary because documentary aims above all else to represent the real: it is not "based on a true story" (a common phrase in film industry advertising); it *is*, it tells us, a true story. Of course, explicitly fictional forms (especially, though not exclusively, those realist in character) also typically make claims of a kind to truth, but these are mediated by the conventions of fiction. The truth claims of documentary are, in this sense, immediate. While fiction's claim to truth may be vulnerable, fiction at least has its more or less acknowledged fictional devices to fall back upon. Documentary stands naked, with its formal devices only so much cause for embarrassment.

But the poststructuralist objection to documentary, while it accurately reveals that the documentary text cannot stand in a simple one-to-one correspondence with the real, fails insofar as it imagines only two possibilities: *either* such a correspondence *or* no correspondence at all. The poststructuralist tendency to deny any correspondence ("The real has nothing to do with it") derives from what Roy Bhaskar has identified as "the epistemic fallacy." According to Bhaskar, the epistemic fallacy results from an illicit identification of what is known about reality with what is real, reducing the real to the known. The version of this fallacy that is especially prevalent in cultural and literary studies is the linguistic fallacy, in which reality is reduced to that which may be said about reality.[12] But knowing (covered by epistemology) and being (covered by ontology) are not identical.

Thus Winston's "marks on the glass" should be seen as an epistemological moment, both hindering and permitting our ability to see—but not preempting the reality of—that which lies on the other side of the glass. As Gary MacLennan writes: "Though the glass is marked, we can see something of the world through it." In a way characteristic of the poststructuralist problematic, the identification of the epistemological moment introduces a radical skepticism about the possibility of *any* access to the real. This in turn logically produces its opposite, the "ontic fallacy," which Bhaskar defines as "the effective ontologization or naturalization of knowledge, the reduction of knowledge to being or its determination by being," a position typical of the traditional defenders of mainstream documentary

---

12. Roy Bhaskar, *A Realist Theory of Science*, 36; *The Possibility of Naturalism: A Philosophical Critique of the Contemporary Human Sciences*, 170–75, 198–200; *Philosophy and the Idea of Freedom*, 140–41. Bhaskar's fundamental point is that being is not reducible to discourse or to knowledge, as may be demonstrated by the fact that the forces described by the causal laws of science act whether people understand them or not. In the realm of the social, similarly, economic forces—though the products of human actions, unlike natural laws—are not dependent upon people understanding them for their operation (see Bhaskar, *Realist Theory of Science*, chap. 1).

practice.[13] In this schema, poststructuralist skepticism and foundational-ist fideism appear to be internally related opposites that insist upon see-ing knowledge as either a "construct" without referential purchase on a merely putative "reality," or as the wholesale incorporation within thought of natural reality. What needs to be rejected here is neither the analysis of the construction of knowledge—the epistemological moment—nor the be-lief in an object independent of thought about which knowledge may be acquired—the ontological moment—but rather the habit of thinking that these moments are irreconcilable.

With regard to documentary, whatever the epistemological problems raised by any given documentary text, the ontological remains prior to it and persists beyond it. Ontologically, reality stands apart from any particu-lar discursive appropriation of it, but it is pervious to certain limited testing procedures, the most powerful of which is scientific experiment. Thus the documentary form, while no guarantor of the truth or utterly transpar-ent window on a readily available objective reality, may provide access to reality, even as it may—and must—also be understood and analyzed in terms of its particular features as a discursive form. As MacLennan notes: "Within [Bhaskar's critical realist] schema it is possible to have epistemo-logical relativism but at the same time to have good reason for selecting one description of reality before another."[14] The critical realist critique of poststructuralism permits the documentary form to serve the function of providing access, partial though it may be, to a reality that is separate from our knowledge of it, as well as from our feelings about it.

Providing such access is precisely the role Rukeyser would have the doc-umentary sections of *The Book of the Dead* play. Each of the major modal groups in the poem—monologue, documentary, and meditation—is prem-ised upon a different relationship between discourse and the reality to which it refers. The monologue refers to a reality that is subjective, in a nonpejorative sense: it attempts to present the truth of its speaker's feelings and thoughts at a moment in time. The documentary refers to an objective reality: it attempts to present the truth of a specific segment of historical and natural reality. The meditation refers to a reality found somewhere beyond the first two: it attempts to present a truth that lies in the realm of historical and natural reality but which requires the mediation of "the subjective factor of the poetical" for its disclosure.[15]

One may see the respective truths of these modal groupings as nested: the first level, the subjective truth of the monologues, is nested within the

13. Gary MacLennan, "From the Actual to the Real: Left Wing Documentary in Aus-tralia 1946–96," 63; Roy Bhaskar, *Reclaiming Reality: A Critical Introduction to Contempo-rary Philosophy*, 157.
14. MacLennan, "From the Actual to the Real," 63.
15. Bloch, "Marxism and Poetry," 160.

objective truth of the documentary poems. That is, the subjective reactions of an Arthur Peyton, feeling he has been wronged, cannot be true or false if confined to their own level. That is how he feels. That he is justified in feeling this way is confirmed in the documentary poems, where the objective conditions in which the tunnel workers labored are presented. And the truth of the documentary poems is in turn nested within the broader perspective of the meditations, which attempt to search out the meanings of what has been revealed in the monologues and documentary poems.

The neatness of the organizing schema just outlined is a product, of course, of analysis, and to that extent belies the real intermixing of forms that takes place in *The Book of the Dead*, as my comments on "Absalom" have demonstrated. Four of the poems already considered might be referred to as documentary in character, though they have been considered under other headings: "West Virginia," "Statement: Philippa Allen," "Mearl Blankenship," and "Absalom." These poems are based upon texts, but with one exception they are used to create an effect sufficiently different from that characteristic of the documentary poems considered in this chapter as to justify their placement elsewhere. "Statement: Philippa Allen" is of a straightforwardly documentary character and is considered within those terms; it is discussed in the chapter on the introductory poems for nongeneric reasons: simply because of its placement in the collection and its crucial role in first mentioning the central facts of the events with which *The Book of the Dead* is concerned.

"West Virginia" is for the most part of a documentary character in that it focuses upon the history of the state and region in which the events of *The Book of the Dead* occurred. Unlike the strictly documentary poems, however, "West Virginia" draws upon a history text rather than a government document, and unlike her practice with regard to the speakers on and before the House subcommittee, Rukeyser makes no effort to reproduce the voice of the historian, Phil Conley. On one level, then, "West Virginia" is of a piece with the other documentary poems in *The Book of the Dead:* its portrait of the state is intended to present a truth about the place in which the Gauley Tunnel tragedy occurred that is not any one person's truth: no engagement with the emotions or subjectivity of a speaker is required of the reader. But whereas the core documentary poems in *The Book of the Dead* reproduce the sound of courtroom testimony and cross-examination, as well as of depositions before the House of Representatives, "West Virginia," while attentive to the sound of a sixteenth- or seventeenth-century exploration narrative or to the inscription on a monument, does not reproduce the documentary source itself at the verbal level.

The title of the sixth poem of *The Book of the Dead*, "Praise of the Committee," is liable to confuse the reader since the committee referred to is not the House subcommittee investigating the Gauley Tunnel tragedy, but rather a local defense committee established by former tunnel workers and local townspeople. This fact is only briefly noted in the poem, but Rukeyser, apparently seeing the possibility for confusion, emphasized it in the script she wrote, in her attempt to have the story of the Gauley Tunnel tragedy made into a film. The defense committee was formed to assist the former workers in coping with, and winning compensation for, their disabilities. This focus on the actions of the former workers and their allies registers a shift from the focus of "Statement: Philippa Allen," which introduced the tunnel project in terms of engineering. "Praise of the Committee" is the first poem in the sequence to consider, in a sustained way, the fate of the workers. Even considered in the most practical terms, this fate was complicated, as the poem indicates, since it involved lawsuits, "crooked lawyers," and intervention, and nonintervention, by state and federal government.[16]

"Praise of the Committee" falls into two parts. The first three-quarters of the poem is the documentary portion, in which Rukeyser draws heavily and freely upon the House transcripts. For roughly the first half of the poem she breaks up the otherwise uninterrupted flow with italicized lines describing, in fragmentary fashion, the defense committee. Between these lines she begins painting a detailed portrait of the disaster, relying most heavily upon the testimony of Philippa Allen. The earliest lines in this portion of the poem bear close scrutiny, since they reveal some of Rukeyser's techniques for increasing the dramatic quality of the testimony, raise questions about the politics of race in the poem, and demonstrate that even in the "minimally poetic" documentary sections, Rukeyser works carefully with the poetic motifs that lend unity to, or "bind," to use Rukeyser's preferred expression, *The Book of the Dead*.[17]

The second and third lines of "Praise of the Committee":

> Almost as soon as work was begun in the tunnel
> men began to die among dry drills. No masks. (77)

are altered from Philippa Allen's testimony:

> These were robust, hard-muscled workmen, and yet many of them began dying almost as soon as the work on the tunnel started.[18]

16. I will discuss the practical affairs of the former workers only to the extent necessary to facilitate understanding of the poem. For further details, see the discussion in Cherniack, *Hawk's Nest Incident*, 52–72, upon which I rely heavily in this section.

17. Rukeyser, interview by Draves and Fortunato, 163.

18. House Subcommittee, *Investigation Relating to Conditions of Workers*, 3.

While not found in this portion of the testimony, references to the use of dry drilling and the absence of protective masks are found throughout the transcript.

What is notable here is Rukeyser's minimal alteration of the testimony for maximal impact: in line 2 she changes the preposition "on" to the more exact and evocative "in" and the verb "started" to the auxiliary construction "was begun," also moving the verb from the terminal to the medial position in the clause. Changing the verb and its location in this way creates an intricate alliterative pattern: the *g*s in "begun," "began," and "among"; the *m*s of "men," "among," and "masks"; and the *d*s of "die," "dry," and "drills." This pattern is strengthened by the conjunction of the tempo-slowing effects of the alliteration of "dry drills" and the heavy pause occasioned by the period that immediately follows, placing great stress on both "No" and especially "masks." Without sacrificing the documentary quality of the lines—and thus the associated value of objective reference—of the lines, Rukeyser lends them a formality they would not otherwise have simply by emphasizing particular aural qualities. The minimal revisions transform them into poetic discourse.

These lines are followed by several taken from elsewhere in Allen's testimony concerning the transitory nature of the workforce assembled to construct the tunnel. Here the focus shifts from the poetic to the political, since here too Rukeyser alters the testimony, but to create a very different effect:

> Most of them were not from this valley.
> The freights brought many every day from States
> all up and down the Atlantic seaboard
> and as far inland as Kentucky, Ohio.   (77)

As does the passage of testimony from which they are taken, these lines describe the influx of migrant workers into Fayette County. But the context, and even to some degree the precise meaning imparted, differs from that in the testimony. Allen's testimony focuses at this point on the treatment accorded the migratory black workers (the lines Rukeyser quotes are in italics):

> We heard of instance after instance of brutal treatment and discrimination. "They was treated worsen if they was mules," Mrs. Jones [the mother of "Absalom"] told us. "The foreman would cuss at them bad and run them ragged. He would run them right back into the powder smoke in the tunnel after a shot, instead of letting them wait 30 minutes like the white men do."
> Why did the Rinehart & Dennis Co., contractors, dare to treat the colored men "worsen if they was mules"? Simply because these poor, ignorant men had no standing in the community and there was no friendly organization to which they could protest. *Most of them were far from home. They had come in droves from States up and down the Atlantic seaboard, from Pennsylvania, Georgia,*

North Carolina, South Carolina, Florida, and from States as far inland as Alabama, Kentucky, Ohio.[19]

Rukeyser's editing of the testimony removes the racial focus, emphasizing instead that many workers were outsiders.

But race was an important element in the Gauley Tunnel tragedy. Not only were migratory black workers placed in the greatest danger inside the tunnel, they were also treated worse than white workers in their housing and other arrangements, as Allen's quotation from Emma Jones suggests. In the work camps built by Rinehart and Dennis, white and black workers alike were housed in two-room, tar-paper shanties. The shanties occupied by whites, however, were provided with electricity, and housed four men. The shanties for blacks were without electricity and housed upwards of ten men. Blacks were also reportedly exposed to a variety of other abuses, although this is subject to dispute.

The racial cast to the Gauley Tunnel tragedy was commented upon, although not extensively, in the testimony before the House subcommittee. Martin Cherniack also explores it in his book *The Hawk's Nest Incident.*[20] But it is less prominent in Rukeyser's poem. While one may assert that the central presence of George Robinson in the poem places the role of black workers in the foreground, it seems more correct to emphasize Rukeyser's relative muting of the racial element in the tragedy. If Rukeyser was aware, from her firsthand experience in Gauley Bridge and her familiarity with the testimony delivered before the House subcommittee, that race was a factor in the tragedy, why does it not enter into *The Book of the Dead* as significantly as it does in Cherniack's book, written in the post–Civil Rights era, and in the testimony of Philippa Allen, upon which Rukeyser drew so heavily?

Two answers seem plausible. First, Rukeyser wrote *The Book of the Dead* during the Popular Front phase of the Communist party. As discussed in Chapter 1, while Rukeyser apparently never joined the party as a member, she belonged to the broad 1930s Left of which the party was an important part, worked for a time for the *Daily Worker,* and appeared frequently in the pages of *New Masses.* It is plausible, then, that Rukeyser deliberately deemphasized the racial dimension of the Gauley Tunnel tragedy under the influence of the Popular Front line, which, to put it briefly, held that the party, rather than seeking to sharply differentiate itself from other political forces in the United States, should seek to forge an alliance with a broad spectrum of nonreactionary elements in the country. This meant toning down the emphasis, characteristic of the party's previous, sectarian Third Period, on a distinctively proletarian culture and backing away from the

19. Ibid., 8–9.
20. Cherniack, *Hawk's Nest Incident,* 17–19, 25–26.

Third Period position on the black population of the United States: that in the "Black Belt," where African Americans formed over half of the population, blacks constituted a separate nation-within-a-nation that should be recognized and politically organized as such. Such ardent black nationalism made for difficult relations with working- and middle-class whites in the South, and was therefore inimical to the line of the Popular Front insofar as it divided rather than united what the party saw as potential allies.[21] By deemphasizing the degree to which race was a factor in the Gauley Tunnel tragedy, Rukeyser emphasized that the victims were, after all, workers, regardless of their race.

The second way of explaining Rukeyser's failure to represent race as a determining factor in the Gauley Tunnel tragedy is more conceptual than political. Rukeyser organized *The Book of the Dead* along lines that are strongly spatial. Indeed, she referred repeatedly in her correspondence to "the Gauley Bridge poems," thus identifying *The Book of the Dead* geographically or spatially rather than otherwise (such as, say, "the silicosis poems").[22] In this regard, it is significant that the sequence begins with "The Road," a poem that draws one's attention to a movement through space that takes one to the place where the tragedy happened. "These are roads to take when you think of your country": the physical placement of the poet (and, by extension, the reader) in the place in which the tragedy occurred serves as the spur to the reflective passages in the poem. Furthermore, Rukeyser accords nature an important place within the poem, and this leads her into a close relation with the land of West Virginia—though Kertesz overstates the case when she claims that the river is "the major character in this drama."[23] So it is that Rukeyser revises the words of Philippa Allen in the way that she does, from "Most of them were far from home" to "Most of them were not from this valley." At the center of Allen's words are the workers and the place they came from ("home"); in Rukeyser's revision the focus is on the workers and the land of the New River gorge.

One consequence of the importance of place in *The Book of the Dead* is that the poem unites the people of the New River valley with the valley

---

21. Barbara Foley summarizes the scholarship on the Communist party's positions on race in *Radical Representations: Politics and Form in U.S. Proletarian Fiction, 1929–1941*, 173–83. She points out that the demand for self-determination in the "Black Belt" was not officially dropped until 1959, although it was "for practical purposes eliminated from the party's mass campaigns, North and South" during the Popular Front (180–81). The international aspect of the Popular Front is well treated in Fernando Claudin, *The Communist Movement: From Comintern to Cominform*, 2:182–99.

22. Rukeyser's son informed me that even when referring in conversation to *The Book of the Dead*, she typically called it "the Gauley Bridge poems." William Rukeyser, interview.

23. Kertesz, *Poetic Vision*, 100.

itself, creating a unified local populace that by turns gains "mastery" and is cheated of this mastery by the forces of corporate capitalism. This, in part, may be seen to motivate the mocking conclusion of "Gauley Bridge":

> What do you want—a cliff over a city?
> A foreland, sloped to sea and overgrown with roses?
> These people live here.   (76)

These lines are, in a sense, false: in many cases "these people," the tunnel workers, worked—and died—there, but did not *live* there.

A further consequence of the emphasis upon place is that the conflict between the outside workers and the local population is muted. Indeed, in choosing as the dominant (white) local voice of "Praise of the Committee" Emma Jones (merged to a degree with her husband Charles), Rukeyser chose a voice that seems to hold not rancor, but rather sympathy, for the sometimes despised black migrants who were most likely to be exposed to the worst conditions. While it may not be said that Rukeyser distorted the situation in Fayette County, her picture here is incomplete, insofar as it does not include the racial antagonism—which *will* surface in "The Cornfield"— between some of the local population and the black workers brought in to drill, blast, and dig through Gauley Mountain.

Curiously enough, if Rukeyser's focus on place in the poem leads her to mute the importance of race and of racial prejudice, it also leads to a certain muting of prejudice based on class that operated within the white community itself. By unifying Gauley Bridge with all of the people who lived there, Rukeyser creates a collective entity, "Gauley Bridge," that is the working class in the poem. While there are also countertendencies that operate against this—the identification of the hotelman and the under-taker as eager accomplices of Union Carbide and Rinehart and Dennis— one strand in the poem does create the impression of a unitary community exploited by outside forces. This, like the muting of racial conflict, might be attributable to the change in the ideological climate of the 1930s with the advent of the Popular Front, for a sharp sense of class conflict could hinder the formation of the broad network that the Communist party was trying to forge.

It would seem, then, that Rukeyser made an artistic choice to organize the poem according to place, emphasizing the spatial or geographical re-lations that obtained in the Gauley Tunnel tragedy. She also made a philo-sophical choice that, while not necessarily entailed by her artistic choice, was certainly compatible with it. This was to emphasize nature as an ob-jective condition in which human subjectivity must find its fulfillment and with which it must try to become reconciled. The artistic and philo-sophical choices Rukeyser made were in keeping with the political climate within which the literary Left worked during the Popular Front era. Thus, the muting of conflict within the population of victims and observers of the Gauley Tunnel tragedy ought to be seen as an effect of the political climate and a correlate of the artistic and philosophical dimensions of the poem.

To return to the individual poem at hand, the final five stanzas of "Praise of the Committee" differ considerably from the previous three-quarters of the poem. In these stanzas, Rukeyser returns to the theme raised toward the end of "West Virginia": the relationship between the power in nature and the power of those whose labor builds the hydroelectric project that harnesses this natural power. The final three stanzas read:

> In this man's face
> family leans out from two worlds of graves—
> here is a room of eyes,
> a single force looks out, reading our life.
>
> Who stands over the river?
> Whose feet go running in these rigid hills?
> Who comes, warning the night,
> shouting and young to waken our eyes?
>
> Who runs through electric wires?
> Who speaks down every road?
> Their hands touched mastery; now they
> demand an answer.   (79)

In the last two stanzas, particularly, the dynamic content and interrogative structure give the lines a fast tempo slowed considerably in the declarative last two lines by the caesura occasioned by the semicolon and by the assonance of three successive syllables in the final line. This shift in tempo emphasizes the introduction of a motif crucial to *The Book of the Dead*: mastery.

The term *mastery*, which occurs in several places in Rukeyser's poem, is another element derived from the Egyptian *Book of the Dead*, where it is used in such formulas as: "I am master of my heart. I am master of my heart-case (or breast). I am master of my arms. I am master of my legs."[24] (As we have seen, the Egyptian *Book of the Dead* figures in "Absalom.") "Their hands touched mastery": not mastery of others, but mastery of their human destiny, mastery of the conditions in which people live. Yet they, who have made this possible, have been denied life itself, and thus "they / demand an answer."

---

24. Budge, *Egyptian Book of the Dead*, 439.

Of course, *mastery* may have sinister connotations in the wake of Hegel's oft-cited "master-slave dialectic" or, more recently, Foucault's investigations of the power/knowledge nexus. Yet Rukeyser's sense of mastery appears to be formulated precisely to distinguish between constructive human power and coercive powers based on hierarchical social structures. Rukeyser's sense of mastery, then, appears to coincide with what Roy Bhaskar designates as a power$_1$ relation, "the transformative capacity intrinsic to the concept of action as such." This contrasts with power$_2$, which is "the capacity to get one's way against either the overt wishes and/or the real interests of others in virtue of structures of exploitation, domination, subjugation, and control."[25] Bhaskar's power$_1$/power$_2$ distinction is crucial to an understanding of Rukeyser's project, since on the one hand "mastery" is a key concept in the poem, and on the other Foucault and his followers have fostered a radical skepticism with regard to power that tends to flatten out distinctions between forms of power. Without some such distinction as Bhaskar's power$_1$-power$_2$, the historical vision and the utopian resonance of *The Book of the Dead* are lost, and with them is lost much of the value of the poem, since Rukeyser's innovative and expert formal devices are in service to them.

Directly following in *The Book of the Dead* the intensely personal "Absalom," "The Disease" (first published in *New Masses*, December 7, 1937) marks a shift into a decidedly documentary mode, one that aims for an objective quality quite distinct from the inwardness associated with lyric expression: the poem is written in the impersonal and scientific voice of a doctor describing the nature and progress of silicosis. In his review of *U.S. 1*, William Carlos Williams appears to have been thinking of this poem in particular when he wrote his most admiring lines:

> She knows how to use the *language* of an x-ray report or a stenographic record of a cross-examination. She knows, in other words, how to select and exhibit her material. She understands what words are for and how important it is not to twist them in order to make "poetry" of them.[26]

Into "the language of an x-ray report" Rukeyser interpolates the voice of one afflicted with silicosis, describing in a more impressionistic and experiential way the sensation of the disease:

> That indicates the progress in ten months' time.
> And now, this year—short breathing, solid scars

25. Roy Bhaskar, *Dialectic: The Pulse of Freedom*, 402.
26. William Carlos Williams, review of *U.S. 1*, 141.

even over the ribs, thick on both sides.
Blood vessels shut. Model conglomeration.

What stage?

Third stage. Each time I place my pencil point:
There and there and there, there, there.

"It is growing worse every day. At night
"I get up to catch my breath. If I remained
"flat on my back I believe I would die."   (83)

But even the introduction of a silicosis victim's voice—drawn from the testimony of George Robison—does not render the poem intimate in the way that "Absalom" is; rather, the poem works precisely because of its objective quality, which helps to make it, in the words of Kertesz, "fraught with more doom than any medieval ballad."[27] Kertesz's astute observation about the tone established by Rukeyser should be supplemented by the reminder that whereas medieval ballads generally understand human affliction as a natural condition, Rukeyser places this sense of doom within the context of a disaster explicitly understood as a product of social (power$_2$) relations.

Like "The Disease," "The Doctors" is drawn from testimony; but where the scientific voice in the first poem offers a noninvidious contrast with the intimate voice found in *The Book of the Dead,* in "The Doctors" Rukeyser appears to chide the medical community for its lack of compassion for the victims of the tragedy—which is to say, for its disinclination to become actively involved in the struggle between Union Carbide and its workers. In the following excerpt—and Rukeyser here draws quite faithfully upon the testimony—an expert witness, Dr. Goldwater, attempts to avoid answering directly the questions put to him. Rukeyser presents Goldwater's overscrupulousness as a shameful indulgence, while the bodies of those who died in the tragedy offer a silent response to the line of questioning.

Dr. Goldwater. First are the factors involving the individual.
                    Under heading B, external causes.
                    Some of the factors which I have in mind—
                    those are the facts upon the blackboard,
                    the influencing and controlling factors.
Mr. Marcantonio. Those factors would bring about acute
                    silicosis?
Dr. Goldwater. I hope you are not provoked when I say "might."
                    Medicine has no hundred percent.
                    We speak of possibilities, have opinions.

27. Kertesz, *Poetic Vision,* 103.

> . . . .
> The man in the white coat is the man on the hill,
> the man with the clean hands is the man with the drill,
> the man who answers "yes" lies still.   (88)

The form of the nursery-rhyme tercet contrasts with the deadly content it conveys, at the same time that it provides a vehicle for the spectral imagery of the last line of the tercet, which paradoxically both departs from the matter-of-factness of "The Doctors" as a whole and asserts that the facts of this case, the reality into which the House members are inquiring, make the most powerful, though in themselves mute, argument of all.

"The Disease: After-Effects" focuses on a character hitherto not present in the poem, Congressman Jerry O'Connell of Montana.[28] After listing some of O'Connell's actions as a representative, Rukeyser shifts to his recollections of his childhood, recollections that give the title of this poem a double meaning. First, the poem is concerned with the after-effects of the disaster as it was made public and investigated by Congress. Second, the poem presents O'Connell's career as itself an after-effect of silicosis:

> This is the gentleman from Montana.
> —I'm a child, I'm leaning from a bedroom window,
> clipping the rose that climbs upon the wall,
> the tea roses, and the red roses,
> one for a wound, another for disease,
> remembrance for strikers. I was five, going on six,
> my father on strike at the Anaconda mine;
> they broke the Socialist mayor we had in Butte,
> the sheriff (friendly), found their judge. Strike-broke.
> Shot father. He died : wounds and his disease.
> My father had silicosis.   (98)

O'Connell preserves the memory of, and acts as far as possible to redeem the life of, his father in his actions as a representative, thus joining the

---

28. Rukeyser explicitly stated that her congressman was "modeled on Jerry O'Connell" in the draft of a letter to Sam and Bella Spewack dated January 2, 1938 (Rukeyser Papers), and in her 1938 radio interview with Samuel Sillen (see Appendix III). In 1937, the *New York Times* carried several stories about O'Connell's actions in Congress: his resolution calling for the pardon of jailed union organizer Tom Mooney ("Asks House Aid Mooney Pardon," March 30, p. 10), regarding an embargo on munitions for Germany and Italy ("Hull Makes Plea to Reich and Spain," June 2, p. 2), and his introduction of an antisilicosis bill ("Anti-Silicosis Bill Filed," July 23, p. 2). With Vito Marcantonio out of Congress between 1936 and 1938, the *Daily Worker* found in O'Connell something of a replacement for its favorite congressman, and featured him in at least a half-dozen stories in the summer of 1937.

mother in "Absalom" as one who struggles against death and injustice. Both cases, that of the son and that of the mother, may be seen as examples of one way in which human being "changes . . . it does not die," as Rukeyser concludes "The Dam," the poem that precedes "The Disease: After-Effects." Rukeyser portrays both the son and the mother as taking up something of the life force of those they love and perpetuating it, so that this force is translated, shifts phases, but does not end.

After this follow three straightforwardly documentary stanzas, largely drawn from testimony. The facts set forward here give rise to the reflections of the next three stanzas, in which O'Connell looks outward from the death of his father to the struggle of the Asturian miners in Spain. These related struggles generate the energy that seeks an outlet in action to protect workers against contracting silicosis:

> and all our meaning lies in this
> signature: power on a hill
> centered in its committee and its armies
> sources of anger, the mine of emphasis. (99)

But this energy, like that of the water flowing through the gorge, is also subject to being checked, if only temporarily:

> It sets up a gradual scar formation;
> this increases, blocking all drainage from the lung,
> eventually scars, blocking the blood supply,
> and then they block the air passageways.
> Shortness of breath,
> pains around the chest,
> he notices lack of vigor.
>
> Bill blocked; investigation blocked.   (99)

Rukeyser sets up a parallel between the progress of silicosis in afflicted lungs, which produces a blockage of the air passages that steadily diminishes the energy of the victim, and the blockage of the bill that would have granted to the subcommittee greater powers of investigation.

In the last stanza, the failure and inaction of Congress calls forth one of the least successful moments in *The Book of the Dead*, in which

> . . . over the country, a million look from work,
> five hundred thousand stand.   (99)

Here, the accusatory looks of those who are or are liable to become victims of silicosis do not appear to be consistent with the larger structure of the poem. The failure of the political system, the blockage, is met with an immediate response that appears wishful on the part of Rukeyser. Elsewhere in *The Book of the Dead* she acknowledges that while defeats may be temporary, they are also real, and the processes of historical unfolding—like the physical forces she describes—work themselves out only in the long run and according to a temporality other than that defined by the length of an individual human life. At the end of "The Disease: After-Effects," Rukeyser apparently fails to stay true to this insight, which otherwise pervades the larger poem.

Yet it is worth questioning whether this way of reading is not overly informed by the subsequent history of the United States, in which it became apparent that the militancy sometimes generated during the 1930s would not translate into a revolutionary movement, nor even seriously threaten the political hegemony of the two major parties. Whatever the limitations of 1930s militancy, workers *could* become actively involved in struggle, especially when it revolved around specific issues, such as silicosis. Perhaps it is best to see the last lines of "The Disease: After-Effects" as a case in point of the difficulty—at times, at least—of distinguishing between aesthetic and historical or political judgment.

"The Bill" is, for most of its length, a rendering into stanzaic form of an edited version of the report filed by the House subcommittee, summarizing its findings and requesting funding and the power of subpoena to enable its further investigation into the Gauley Tunnel disaster. It was the denial of this request that blocked further investigation. But at the end of "The Bill," as at the end of "The Disease: After-Effects," Rukeyser reminds us that ends are always, in a sense, illusions:

> Words on a monument.
> Capitoline thunder. It cannot be enough.
> The origin of storms is not in clouds,
> our lightning strikes when the earth rises,
> spillways free authentic power:
> dead John Brown's body walking from a tunnel
> to break the armored and concluded mind. (102)

This resonates powerfully within the framework of *The Book of the Dead* as a whole. The metaphor of the storm appears to present a materialist theory of history through a poetic figure: social movements are not created by politics; rather, politics is a response to developments "on the ground." Indeed, the hydrological cycle provides a resource upon which Rukeyser draws again in "The Dam," where she offers a vision of history intricately worked out in the language of this metaphor.

The image of a resurrected John Brown connects with a number of other images throughout the poem: the unnamed indentured servant, and Brown himself, in "West Virginia"; the family—especially Shirley—of Emma Jones in "Absalom"; Jerry O'Connell's father in "The Disease: After-Effects," and the buried tunnel workers of "The Cornfield," to name the most prominent. The latent meaning of Brown and the other figures with whom he resonates connects with the historical tendency Rukeyser traces throughout *The Book of the Dead*, as the image of resurrection serves as a figure of the ineluctable force that underlies human history: the drive to humanize the conditions of existence, the drive for mastery, the utopian drive.

The Book of the Dead is composed of elements associated with the traditional genre divisions: the tripartite classification of epic, lyric, and dramatic. It should be understood, then, as the result of a combinatory practice that is by its nature experimental. Having examined the first two generic elements, epic and lyric, I want now to defend explicitly the importance of a generic analysis of *The Book of the Dead*. The full significance of Rukeyser's experimentation with poetic genres is best illuminated by the genre theory of Hegel, as set forward in his *Aesthetics*, and by the more recent work of Emil Staiger in his *Basic Concepts of Poetics*. Both Hegel and Staiger develop their theories on the basis of the tripartite division of the genres; yet, while a rough synthesis of Hegel and Staiger underpins the fundamental analysis undertaken in this book, Hegel's *Aesthetics* differs significantly from Staiger's *Basic Concepts*, particularly in Hegel's placement of the epic prior to the lyric as a necessary precondition. This appears theoretically, sociologically, and historically to be correct, whereas Staiger's existentialist placement of the lyric prior to the epic and the subject/object split seems to me dubious.

Staiger is especially useful, however, in that he understands the genres as elements rarely if ever found in their pure state. Poems are composed of a combination of generic elements, just as secondary colors are made up of combinations of primary colors. Thus, for Staiger, the classic three-fold distinction between the lyric, the epic, and the dramatic designates the fundamental elements that are present in any poetic work in varying proportions, rather than distinct genres into which works in their entirety fall: "Every poetic creation takes part—to a larger or smaller degree—in all three genre concepts."[29]

Furthermore, despite their differences, Hegel and Staiger agree as to the major characteristics of the various genres. *Epical*, for Hegel, refers to a mode that "presents what is itself objective in its objectivity" and for Staiger "is entirely a matter of elucidating, of showing, of making things visible."

---

29. Emil Staiger, *Basic Concepts of Poetics*, 93.

To Hegel, *lyrical* refers to a mode in which "the centre of the thing is not the occurrence itself but the state of mind which is mirrored in it," while Staiger understands the lyrical as "a rendering of the soul in words." To Hegel, *dramatic* refers to a mode that "conjoins the two previous [modes] into a new whole in which we see in front of us both an objective development and also its origin in the hearts of individuals." In addition to this synthetic function, the dramatic is also the privileged form for the depiction of conflict, "the discord and contradiction of opposing dispositions, aims, and activities which absolutely demands resolution and presses on towards this result." Staiger efficiently characterizes the dramatic mode with the term *tension*. The three modes, whether we use Hegel's or Staiger's terminology, stand for distinct relations to the world: the lyric is the mode of "remembrance"; the epic, the mode of "presentation"; the dramatic, of "tension."[30]

With this sense of the basic poetic modes of *The Book of the Dead* established, we may more clearly see the problem that Rukeyser addresses. The lyrical mode in itself tends toward a kind of hermeticism, to offer value without fact; the documentary mode in itself tends toward barrenness, to offer fact without value. As Adorno puts it: "A totally objectivated artwork would congeal into a mere thing, whereas if it altogether evaded objectivation it would regress into an impotently powerless subjective impulse and flounder in the empirical world." Rukeyser attempts to unite these sundered terms of modernity without simply declaring them united and without denying that they are sundered, using a procedure that contrasts with the attempt of the romantics to heal, in Abrams's words, "the cleavage between subject and object, between the vital, purposeful, value-full world of private experience and the dead postulated world of extension, quantity, and motion" via the poet's subjectivity.[31]

Rather than establishing the terms of one side of this divide as paramount, Rukeyser produces a text in which the documentary poems are counteracted by the interiority upon which the monologues are predicated, while the monologues are offset by the discipline of the outward reality to which the documentary poems are servant. This procedure permits the object its moment of truth in the documentary poems, and the subject its moment in the monologues, before they are brought together at a higher level of abstraction in the meditative poems. Thus, while the documentary form was meant as a corrective to the overly inward focus of the postromantic lyric, Rukeyser's use of it does not simply cancel out this inwardness.

---

30. G. W. F. Hegel, *Aesthetics: Lectures on Fine Art*, 2:1037–38, 1116, 1168; Staiger, *Basic Concepts of Poetics*, 93, 104.

31. T. W. Adorno, *Aesthetic Theory*, 175; M. H. Abrams, *The Mirror and the Lamp: Romantic Theory and the Critical Tradition*, 65.

Rather, she attempts to retain the subjective richness of lyric expression at the same time that she confronts it with an objective reality that the lyric all too easily skirts. In the meditative poems, *The Book of the Dead* explores the transindividual meaning of an event—the Gauley Tunnel tragedy—that occurred in the world of outward reality.

4

The Meditations
and a Coda

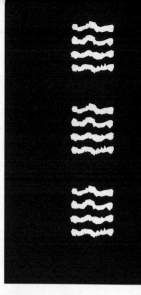

In the previous chapter I asserted that the meditative poems of *The Book of the Dead* display key features of what Hegel and Emil Staiger consider the dramatic element in poetry. Since nothing could appear less dramatic than meditation, a closer examination of this is in order. Whereas *lyric* refers to that in a literary text which is "at one with itself" and *epic* refers to that which is simply present before the eye of the beholder, *dramatic* refers to that which is neither at one with itself nor—because it is radically incomplete—fully present before the beholder. While it lacks the lyric's emphasis on "remembrance" and the epic's emphasis on "presentation," the dramatic features "tension." More specifically, the tension characteristic of Hegel's and Staiger's conception of the dramatic may be broken down into four elements: distance, conflict, argument, and judgment, all of which may be found in the meditative poems of *The Book of the Dead*.

Distance refers to the separation of subject and object characteristic of the dramatic. In Staiger's schema, this separation is not present in the lyric and is only partially advanced in the epic:

> In the lyric realm there is not yet any distance between subject and object. The "I" swims along in the transience of things. In the epic the subject-object dichotomy comes into being. With the act of looking the object becomes firm at the same time as does the "I" looking at this object. Yet subject and object are still bound to one another in the act of showing themselves and of look-ing. . . . But in dramatic existence on the other hand the object is put more or less *ad acta*. Here, we do not observe; rather, we judge. The measure, the meaning, the order that always revealed themselves to the observer in rela-tion to objects and people during his epic wanderings is now in the drama separated from the object world and is grasped and asserted in itself, in the abstract.[1]

1. Staiger, *Basic Concepts of Poetics*, 181–82.

While the monologues of *The Book of the Dead* present the various states of mind of their speakers, and when they call for judgment (as, for example, in "Absalom") do so on a case-by-case basis, the meditative poems move beyond the experiences of any particular individual, using the monologues as data or particulars in the exposition of a more general argument. Hence the key meditative sequence of "Alloy," "Power," and "The Dam" draws away from the specific individuals of the monologues and plays itself out in a dialectical movement in which the experience of these individuals is presented as part of an unfolding history of humanity, a perspective sufficiently abstract that the lyrical monologue is inadequate to its articulation.

The distance between subject and object permitted and presupposed by the dramatic lends it to depicting conflict, something that the epic also would appear to incline toward. But as Staiger astutely notes, it is doubtful that conflict as such is at the center of epic, which uses conflict (between Greeks and Trojans, for example) as an occasion for the display or presentation of the things of this world, to which the epic is truly dedicated. The thoroughgoing nature of the epic concern with the individuality of things contributes to its accretive structure, whereby episodes may be included or excluded without materially affecting the whole, and to the particular way in which it depicts conflict, whereby war is reduced to a series of individual combats. Because the epic, in Staiger's sense, is so closely tied to the individual things and beings of the world, it is profoundly concrete. However, this concreteness operates as a limit with regard to war as a poetic subject. As Staiger puts it, "Nothing is more foreign to the Homeric hero than an ideological war."[2] An ideological war is based on a transindividual, abstract principle that motivates, justifies, and explains individual acts. The epic, restricted to the things of the world and their presentation, cannot depict argument but only collision.

It falls to the dramatic element to present conflict not as collision, but rather as a form of argument. And in presenting a form of argument, it calls on the reader not only to sympathize or to observe but also to judge:

> The measure, the meaning, the order that always revealed themselves to the observer in relation to objects and people during his epic wanderings is now in the drama separated from the object world and is grasped and asserted in itself, in the abstract.[3]

The dramatic element, in Staiger's sense, can be demonstrated to be omnipresent in Rukeyser's poetry, finding frequent expression in her characteristic use of the language of war. Thus it is not surprising in an extended

2. Ibid., 125.
3. Ibid., 182.

work such as *The Book of the Dead* that an already present conflict should find expression both as an element in individual poems and in a series of poems dedicated to conflict as such. If this categorization of the meditative poems is correct, their function within *The Book of the Dead* becomes clear: they perform an act, essentially, of dialectical synthesis. They take up the individual lives and perspectives of the monologues and the factual presentations of the documentary poems, subject them to interpretation, and render a verdict not only on the Gauley Tunnel tragedy but also on that aspect of a broader human history of which it is a part. The reality about which the meditative poems speak lies at a level deeper than that which may simply be presented; it must be argued for.

The Meditations

The first of the meditative poems, "The Cornfield" (first published in *New Masses*, December 7, 1937),[4] is in its own way fully as impressive as the centerpiece of the monologues, "Absalom." Alternating between the documentary mode, which draws once again from testimony delivered before the House subcommittee, and the meditative style, "The Cornfield" establishes the tone that characterizes the major meditative sequence of "Alloy," "Power," and "The Dam." However, the shift toward the meditative does not indicate a drawing away from the Gauley Tunnel tragedy as the subject of the poem; rather, Rukeyser—implicitly acknowledging that the meditative tradition in poetry generally operates by means of a withdrawal from the "sordid" materiality with which she is concerned—calls on "those given to contemplation" to contemplate in detail the horror that took place in Fayette County. Similarly, she calls on "those who like ritual" and "those given to voyages" to focus their attention on the near-at-hand, on what has transpired here, in a prosaic West Virginia county. Thus "The Cornfield" mixes a contemplative, at times nearly dreamlike, mood and tone with the stark facts (and, in one instance, a false rumor) about the conditions under which about forty-five of the tunnel workers died and were buried.

While "The Cornfield" is directly concerned with the events that occurred in Fayette County, it also contains the most allusive of Rukeyser's writing in *The Book of the Dead*. Rukeyser uses allusion to attack the poetry and sensibility of Archibald MacLeish. As Louise Kertesz points out, the by-now-familiar conclusion of "Gauley Bridge" ("What do you want—a

---

4. As it appears in *New Masses*, "The Cornfield" contains one less line than does the version in *U.S. 1* and *Collected Poems*. It is the thirty-third line of the poem: "His mother is suing him : misuse of land," following the lines "Rinehart & Dennis paid him $55 / a head for burying these men in plain pine boxes."

cliff over a city? / A foreland, sloped to sea and overgrown with roses? / These people live here") is a response to the romantic intoxication with more lovely foreign places in MacLeish.[5] In "American Letter," MacLeish wrote of his reluctant return to the United States after several years in Paris:

> This land is my native land. And yet
> I am sick for home for the red roofs and the olives,
> And the foreign words and the smell of the sea fall.
> . . . .
> We are sick at heart for the red roofs and the olives.[6]

But Rukeyser's most pointed and significant critique—not only of Mac-Leish, but also of an entire poetic sensibility—is found in "The Cornfield," which attacks MacLeish's long poem *The Pot of Earth* (1925).

The tone and technique of *The Pot of Earth* derive from Eliot's *Waste Land* and are quite likely also informed by Eliot's essay on Joyce's *Ulysses*.[7] The influence of Eliot, widely noted in criticism on MacLeish, is visible in the headnote from Sir James Frazer's *Golden Bough;* in the poem's concern with "the dead god"; in the diction ("tuber," "breeding," and so on); in the use of specific place-names without providing a more general, orienting context; in the use of colloquial language to convey callousness and incomprehension ("Ripe as a peach she is"); and in the device of appending to a passage an arresting and surprising question, an apparent non sequitur, directed at the reader. Following the Eliotic pattern, *The Pot of Earth* juxtaposes the myth of Adonis with the life story of a young woman of the contemporary world, constructing a myth of thwarted or, more accurately, destructive fertility: the Adonis myth contrasts with the tale of the woman, whose fertility proves her downfall when she dies as a result of giving birth. If anything, MacLeish is even bleaker than Eliot. Unlike *The Waste Land*, *The Pot of Earth* appears to offer no possible or potential redemption, however remote or unrealizable, for the blight it figures, and the fate of the young woman is literally *her fate:* she is presented as having forebodings about fertility even as a young girl, and she is the only character with any substantial existence in the poem. Yet while she is granted by far the fullest development of any figure in the poem, she is utterly subordinate to her function: to be the bearer and victim of fertility.

5. Kertesz, *Poetic Vision*, 101. A more mature MacLeish is ably described and defended by John Timberman Newcomb in his essay "Archibald MacLeish and the Poetics of Public Speech: A Critique of High Modernism." Newcomb focuses on MacLeish's career in the 1930s and, to a lesser extent, in the post–World War II era. While Rukeyser was decidedly to the left of MacLeish, her estimate of his work was not wholly negative, as shown by her review of *Land of the Free* in the *New Masses*.

6. Archibald MacLeish, *Poems, 1924–1933*, 161–62, 164.

7. T. S. Eliot, "*Ulysses*, Order, and Myth."

Rukeyser's desire to counter MacLeish's poem likely arose from at least two sources. First, *The Pot of Earth,* like *The Waste Land* (and, if we follow Eliot's reading of it, *Ulysses*) before it, uses mythic construction to remove events from a social and historical context, placing them instead in a realm supposedly timeless. The effect, in MacLeish's poem at least, of such a strategy is to aestheticize events and emotions: the depiction of the doomed young woman is in a sense the very type of the "purposiveness without a purpose" called for in Kantian aesthetics.[8] In opposition to this, in *The Book of the Dead* Rukeyser confronts events of the historical world, whose meaning is to be found in that world; more generally, Rukeyser's understanding of the poetic imagination invariably joined it with the historical project of civilization. Rukeyser's second motive for going after MacLeish was simply that he was representative, in Dwight Macdonald's words, of poetry of an "officially established" kind, against which Rukeyser was, in part, writing even as she appropriated elements from it. Hence MacLeish may be taken to represent the "establishment culture," or at least its aesthetically advanced section, and so to be complicit with a reality whose sinister political character Rukeyser exposes in her poem. MacLeish's status as an "officially established" poet made him subject also to attacks from leftist writers Granville Hicks, Kenneth Patchen, Mike Gold, and Robert Gorham Davis.[9]

The first section of *The Pot of Earth* is entitled "The Sowing of the Dead Corn," which must have struck Rukeyser as fortuitous (despite *corn* being used in the sense of "wheat"), since the mythic qualities of *The Pot of Earth* contrast so sharply with the gritty reality that Rukeyser encountered in West Virginia and wanted to convey in her poem. While the corn of MacLeish's poem is fodder for mythic construction, Rukeyser's cornfield is a specific cornfield with a precise significance: it belonged to the mother of undertaker Hadley C. White and was where the bodies of at least forty-five tunnel workers were expeditiously buried. White was paid $55 apiece for disposing of the corpses, when the normal payment for a pauper's burial was $30.[10]

The first two stanzas of "The Cornfield" contrast two scenes. In the first stanza, the reader is presented with the interior of the home of an unnamed man:

8. Immanuel Kant, *Critique of Judgment,* 77.

9. Macdonald's comment may be found in Kertesz, *Poetic Vision,* 180 n. MacLeish is skewered with varying degrees of insight in Granville Hicks [Margaret Wright Mather, pseud.], "Der Shöne Archibald"; Kenneth Patchen, "The Old Lean over the Tombstones"; Mike Gold, "Out of the Fascist Unconscious"; and Robert Gorham Davis [Obed Brooks, pseud.], "Archibald MacLeish." It is some indication of the political volatility of the 1930s that by the time of *The Book of the Dead,* MacLeish, as well as Rukeyser, was publishing in *New Masses.*

10. Cherniack, *Hawk's Nest Incident,* 59–60.

> For those given to contemplation : this house,
> wading in snow, its cracks are sealed with clay,
> walls papered with print, newsprint repeating,
> in-focus grey across the room, and squared
> ads for a book : HEAVEN'S MY DESTINATION,
> HEAVEN'S MY . . . HEAVEN. . . . THORNTON WILDER.[11]   (89)

Rukeyser depicts the kind of domestic interior to which she would return in a 1939 photo-essay for *Coronet*, "Adventures of Children," for which she supplied the text. The photo-essay includes a photograph by Carl Mydans, a Resettlement Administration photographer, that shows a young girl standing in a room whose walls are papered with newsprint. This photo-essay and another she published in *Coronet*, "Worlds Alongside," juxtapose scenes from opposite sides of the American economic spectrum.

This juxtaposition structures the first two stanzas of "The Cornfield," as the second stanza presents the world of Hadley C. White and begins in earnest the assault on MacLeish:

> Swear by the corn,
> the found-land corn, those who like ritual. *He*
> rides in a good car. They say blind corpses rode
> with him in front, knees broken into angles,
> head clamped ahead.   (89)

The first two lines contain three digs at MacLeish: "Swear by the corn" mocks both the use of "the dead corn" in *The Pot of Earth* and MacLeish's "The Hamlet of A. MacLeish," which, like Shakespeare's play, features a ghost commanding, "Swear!"; "the found-land corn" mocks the title of MacLeish's 1930 volume, *New Found Land*, in which "American Letter" appeared; and "those who like ritual" mocks the use of ancient myths merely to supply aesthetic pleasure while simultaneously evading historical reality, as in *The Pot of Earth*.

Rukeyser contrasts the life of the undertaker with both the life of the man depicted in the first stanza and with the deaths of the workers he helped

---

11. While presumably based on something Rukeyser saw in the course of her visit to Gauley Bridge in 1936, the reference to Thornton Wilder's 1935 novel, *Heaven's My Destination*, suggests Mike Gold's attack on Wilder in 1930, "Wilder: Prophet of the Genteel Christ." In *Left Letters : The Culture Wars of Mike Gold and Joseph Freeman*, James D. Bloom sees Gold's attacks on Wilder and MacLeish as closely linked (55–57). Like MacLeish, Wilder represented a more staid and established literary culture than that of Rukeyser and Gold, although Rukeyser, because of her own privileged background, could not share wholeheartedly in Gold's proletarian contempt for Wilder's and MacLeish's Ivy League pedigrees.

bury.[12] White's office not only contrasts with the home depicted in the first stanza, it also contains within itself the rankings of class, which stay with us, it seems, even unto death; the coffins are available "satin-lined, silk-lined, unlined, cheap." And of course White offers the opinion that the men he buried were merely "Negroes who got wet at work, / shot craps, drank and took cold, pneumonia, died." Against the easy dismissal of the tunnel workers made by one who profited from their deaths, Rukeyser will balance in the second half of "The Cornfield" a quasi-mythic view that characterizes these men quite differently.

The last three stanzas of "The Cornfield" alternate between lines derived from the testimony of the former tunnel worker George Robison, descriptions of the cornfield, and reflections on the significance of its crop. Rukeyser generates in these stanzas a kind of mythology of redemption in which the dead and buried workers become something like the slain god of which Eliot makes such famous use. Yet Rukeyser's "mythology," in which the dead workers threaten to rise up, is anchored by the more humble reality expressed in the lines, taken from testimony, that begin and end the following excerpt, which closes the poem:

> Do they seem to fear death?
> Contemplate.
> Does Mellon's ghost[13] walk, povertied at last,
> walking in furrows of corn, still sowing,

12. Rukeyser repeats rumors that appear to have been false: White seems to have buried each worker separately in his own coffin, and not to have broken limbs in order to fit stiffened corpses into his car (Cherniack, *Hawk's Nest Incident*, 59–60).

13. "Mellon's ghost" apparently refers to Andrew William Mellon (1855–1937). Secretary of the treasury under presidents Harding, Coolidge, and Hoover, he was a member of the wealthy and powerful Mellon family. The family owned the Pittsburgh Coal Company, which attempted to break the United Mine Workers in the late 1920s. While of national prominence, the Mellons were based in Pittsburgh and thus particularly important in the region that includes West Virginia. Though Rukeyser may not have been aware of Mellon's remarks to the National Electric Light Association, they are ironic given what the Gauley Tunnel tragedy revealed: "Both labor and capital are beginning to realize that they have common interests in building up great industries which are sources of wealth for all and that in America, with the opportunities it offers and the constant transition from poverty to wealth, there is no place for class antagonisms or class warfare" (quoted in Harvey O'Connor, *Mellon's Millions: The Biography of a Fortune; The Life and Times of Andrew W. Mellon,* 339). Mellon died on August 27, 1937, while Rukeyser was working on *The Book of the Dead*. His death occasioned several critical articles in the *Daily Worker,* including a two-part series by Art Shields ("Hearst and Mellon Were Partners in Robbing U.S. of Millions in Taxes," "Mellon Bootlegged While Secretary of Treasury," September 2–3). Interestingly, another story published in the *Daily Worker* ("U of P Editor Defended for Mellon Attack," October 2, 1937) refers to "Andrew Mellon's ghost," which, the story says, "still reigns at the University of Pittsburgh's cathedral of learning."

do apparitions come?
Voyage.
Think of your gardens. But here is corn to keep.
Marked pointed sticks to name the crop beneath.
Sowing is over, harvest is coming ripe.

—No, sir; they want to go on.
They want to live as long as they can.   (90)

Rukeyser contrasts the highly formal, incantatory lines that conclude the next-to-last stanza and the two informal lines that conclude the poem. She structures the last three lines of the penultimate stanza with distinct care. Each line is end-stopped, and each features a strong pause in the middle, a pause that in the first two lines coincides with a shift from an irregular meter in the first half of the line to the succession of three regular iambs in the second half. The terminal assonance of "keep" and "beneath" further heightens the sense of formality.

The contrast between these lines and the informal "No, sir; they want to go on. / They want to live as long as they can" efficiently presents the poles between which the second half of "The Cornfield" oscillates: that of a mythology of the martyred workers (which, when fully elaborated in "The Dam," will figure their rebirth via a historical process through which their class seizes control of human destiny, in the moment of the "harvest . . . coming ripe") and that of the ordinary individual worker, who has no desire to be a slain god. Without, then, transforming these workers into allegorical figures who lose all human particularity beneath the weight of the framework they must bear—the kind of allegorizing against which Georg Lukács protests so powerfully in his attacks on modernism—Rukeyser introduces a meaning-giving framework, one that operates in tandem with, not in opposition to, history.[14]

Rukeyser's willingness and ability to refunction the mythological for leftist poetic use is remarkable in light of the fact that the opposition between the mythic and the historical—and, by extension, between the mythic and the modern, and the mythic and the ideological—is a common feature of a diverse body of writing on myth. For MacLeish, as for many modernists, Eliot made the case most powerfully for myth as an alternative to history in his comments on *Ulysses*. Eliot held that the method of "manipulating a continuous parallel between contemporaneity and antiquity" disclosed by Joyce offered "a way of controlling, of ordering, of giving a shape and a significance to the immense panorama of futility and anarchy which is contemporary history."[15] Myth, or rather this mythical method,

---

14. See Lukács' still provocative essay, "The Ideology of Modernism" (1957).
15. Eliot, "*Ulysses*, Order, and Myth," 270.

provides an alternative to history—the opposition could not be clearer—and a brief look at *The Waste Land* (and Pound's *Cantos*) throws into relief Rukeyser's distinctive use of mythological materials and methods.

While James Longenbach argues that Eliot's comment on *Ulysses* does not, as it is often held to, illuminate *The Waste Land* so much as it does "The Hollow Men" and *Four Quartets*, it does express one powerful tendency in *The Waste Land:* that toward the unification of a fragmented reality, with a simultaneous displacement of history, all through the agency of myth. Insofar as this fragmentation is understood as a historical phenomenon, coinciding with the replacement of the Church-centered past by capitalist modernity, the function of the mythical method remains that of presenting an alternative to history. If *The Waste Land* is less univocal than the *Ulysses* essay in its assertion of mythic order, this is in part a function of the difference, emphasized by Frank Lentricchia, between Eliot's supremely confident prose and his anxiety-ridden poetry, as well as of the difference between the young Eliot and the slightly older Eliot who was attempting "to impose an order on a body of work that he desperately wanted to leave behind him."[16] Thus the essay's closer fit with "The Hollow Men" and *Four Quartets*. What Eliot wanted to leave behind him appears to have been the tensions and contradictions that arose in *The Waste Land*, contradictions and tensions that, it can be argued, bespoke all too accurately the lived reality of post–World War I Europe, to say nothing of Eliot's personal life, and which the mythical method was unable ultimately to resolve.

Of course, despite Eliot's attempt to elevate myth over history in the *Ulysses* essay, in a sense *The Waste Land* does engage its contemporary situation profoundly, emerging from the spiritual desolation of post–World War I Europe—or, in a somewhat longer view, from the modern world as it developed following the election in 1829 of Andrew Jackson, which, Eliot averred, ended his family's America.[17] Yet at the same time, when "Red sullen faces sneer and snarl / From doors of mudcracked houses" (lines 344–45), we get a poetic fantasy, while the more densely social portraiture of the "Game of Chess" section is too reduced, too concentrated on single moments in sordid modern life as it is found in the upper and lower classes—without any exploration of those lives in their totality—to elicit anything more than a half-pleasurable shudder at this image of spiritual desolation. In what might be regarded as a symptomatic moment in the composition of *The Waste Land*, explicit reference to the contemporary political scene was eliminated. The "hooded hordes swarming / Over endless

---

16. James Longenbach, *Modernist Poetics of History: Pound, Eliot, and the Sense of the Past*, 202–3; Lentricchia, *Modernist Quartet*, 278–79.

17. This comment appears in a letter to Stephen Spender quoted in Spender, "Remembering Eliot," 76.

plains" (lines 369–70) in the published version of the poem were originally swarming over "Polish plains," a clear reference to the Russo-Polish war of 1920, fought between the newly founded Soviet Union and the newly restored state of Poland, which was attempting to reclaim its eighteenth-century frontiers. The Red Army approached the limits of Warsaw before being forced to retreat.[18]

Eliot did, to some degree, restore this historical reference when he added notes for the book publication of the poem. The note to the section we are concerned with quotes from Herman Hesse's *Blick ins Chaos* (A glimpse into chaos):

> Already is half of Europe, already is at least half of Eastern Europe, on the way to chaos, riding drunkenly in holy madness into the abyss and singing, singing drunken hymns as Dmitri Karamazov sang. Over these songs laughs the bourgeois, offended; the saint and seer hear them with tears.[19]

Even so, Eliot did not restore the specificity of the original line, whereby socialist revolution clearly figures as the force that threatens to take London the way of Jerusalem, Athens, and Vienna.

Artistically, of course, the excision of the specific place-name, with or without the footnote, makes great sense: the revised line presents a generalized vision of civilization imperiled that is more compatible with the poem's evocation of the Grail myth than is the ideologically pointed line in the draft. The gloss by Grover Smith, who is more than familiar with the sources of the poem, on lines 367–77 of *The Waste Land* demonstrates this:

> On the plains are "hooded hordes," partly barbarians from the steppes, threatening to sweep over Europe, partly Tibetan tribesmen, perpetuating after a fashion the traditions of Buddhism. The nightmare of civilization in chaos mingles with a view of falling churches in the unreal cities. The Grail Chapel falls as the religious and cultural capitals are falling, the cities of the plain.[20]

The ultimate imprecision of these figures is the result of Eliot's substitution of "endless" for "Polish," excising the line's overt historical and political content. In regard to Eliot, then, it appears that Philip Rahv was essentially correct when he asserted, "What the craze for myth represents most of all is the fear of history."[21]

---

18. Eric Hobsbawm, *The Age of Extremes*, 70.

19. T. S. Eliot, "Notes on *The Waste Land*," in *Collected Poems, 1909–1962*, 75. A negative assessment of the effect of this reassertion of the political and social can be found in Grover Smith's comment: "The citation in the 'Notes' (lines 367–77) of Herman Hesse's *Blick ins Chaos* . . . represents Eliot's moralizing in the social dimension" (Smith, *The Waste Land*, 119).

20. Smith, *Eliot's Poetry*, 94.

21. Philip Rahv, *The Myth and the Powerhouse: Essays on Literature and Ideas*, 7.

Yet *The Waste Land*, as Franco Moretti argues, can be resolved into neither the absolute closure of myth nor the endless play of fragments; or, more accurately, it can be resolved in either direction, as the poem offers both possibilities.[22] For example, the poem's mythic dimension accounts for the restriction of the poem's characters to roles, whereby their function is to manifest certain permanent features, as opposed to novelistic characters, who are capable of change. In this regard, the mythic structure of *The Waste Land* closes the multiple possibilities opened up by the text, and the work as a whole tends toward the univocal.

At the same time *The Waste Land* is a collection of heterogeneous fragments, seemingly capable of being substituted for unto infinity, a characteristic that is utterly *un*mythic, since, as Levi-Strauss has shown, primitive myths, as opposed to modernist literary myths, are absolutely binding in terms of their elements. Moretti makes the audacious suggestion that in its utter promiscuity of reference *The Waste Land*, that beacon of high culture, prefigured the mass culture of the post–World War II world.[23] Since it exists simultaneously at these two levels, one might well see *The Waste Land* as in tension between unity, order, and the mythic at one pole, and fragmentation, "chaos," and history at the other, or to think of the poem tending in these two directions at once, toward concentration and dispersal, unity and fragmentation, and so on. But whatever its success or failure, the task of the mythical method remains to restore order and a sense of the sacred, to stem the flow of profane history.

It is, of course, difficult to discuss *The Waste Land* without mentioning Ezra Pound, though if *The Waste Land* presents grave dangers to anyone who attempts to treat it briefly, the wisdom of treating the *Cantos* briefly is questionable indeed. While *The Waste Land* consists of 433 densely allusive lines, plus notes, the *Cantos* run to over 800 pages, each filled with densely allusive lines. Yet Pound's great attempt to revive and revise the epic poem in modern conditions almost certainly exerted a direct influence on Rukeyser's poem, even if that influence is not, as yet, provable (as discussed in Chapter 3). Michael Thurston sees Pound's version of documentary poetics as closely related to, though hardly the same as, those of Rukeyser in *The Book of the Dead*.[24] Indeed, Rukeyser's poem is as clearly written in the wake of the *Cantos* as is William Carlos Williams's *Paterson* and Louis Zukofsky's *A*.[25] Therefore, in order to indicate some of the crucial

---

22. Moretti, "From *The Waste Land* to the Artificial Paradise."

23. Ibid., 228–39.

24. Thurston, "Documentary Modernism," 73–74.

25. Williams's biographer Paul Mariani suggests that *Paterson* should also be seen as being written in the wake of *The Book of the Dead*, since Williams wrote his review of it while he was "looking for leads for his new work" (*William Carlos Williams: A New World Naked*, 417).

differences between *The Book of the Dead* and its poetic precursor without which—in some sense, at least—it could not have been written, it is necessary to look again at Pound.

Out of the intimidating bulk of Pound's *Cantos*, one can find a particularly salient point of comparison with Rukeyser's poem in Canto 41. This canto is, like *The Book of the Dead*, in part concerned with a technological achievement. On the basis of this simple (perhaps simple-minded) similarity, we can isolate and compare some further aspects of the two poets. Canto 41 begins with the much commented-upon scene of Italy's fascist dictator, Mussolini, complimenting the poet on *A Draft of XXX Cantos*, a copy of which Pound had sent him in advance of their meeting.[26] Pound goes on to praise Mussolini for the draining of the Pontine and other marshes in northern Italy, a project that had been contemplated as far back as the days of the Roman Empire:

> "MA QVESTO,"
>   said the Boss, "è divertente."
> catching the point before the aesthetes had got
>   there;
> Having drained off the muck by Vada
> From the marshes, by Circeo, where no one else wd. have
>   drained it.
> Waited 2000 years, ate grain from the marshes;
> Water supply for ten million, another one million *"vani"*
> that is rooms for people to live in.
>   XI of our era.   (*Cantos*, 202)

These two episodes, Mussolini's meeting with the poet and his draining of the marsh, are for Pound related: Mussolini's ability—as Pound sees it—to cut to the heart of the matter of the *Cantos* is comparable to his ability to bring to completion a project long-contemplated, but upon which no one had ever been willing or able to act. In this sense, the draining of the swamp is important primarily as an index of Mussolini's greatness, just as in the Malatesta Cantos (Cantos 8–11) the construction of the grand, if flawed, temple dedicated to St. Francis, the Tempio, is a sign of the greatness of the Renaissance condottiere Sigismundo Malatesta. But as with the Tempio, the drained swamp is also a symbol of redeemed space, of land wrested from chaos, lent order and placed within the productive and meaningful schema of human life.[27]

---

26. Noel Stock, *The Life of Ezra Pound*, 306.

27. For the marsh-draining project, see Carroll F. Terrell, *A Companion to* The Cantos *of Ezra Pound*, 167; Ezra Pound, *Jefferson and/or Mussolini: L'idea Statale; Fascism as I Have Seen It*, 23.

For Pound, the draining of the marshes is primarily a feat of the will of a strong leader; it is not a sign primarily of progress, nor of the increasing power of humans to control the world in which they live. Indeed, insofar as Mussolini's accomplishments may be compared to Sigismundo Malatesta's or Thomas Jefferson's (as Pound does in *Jefferson and/or Mussolini*), they are located within a kind of "perennial history" in which the great leader, the strong man, rises above the masses and above mere circumstance to leave a mark on history. Pound's concern with the recurrent has been noted by critics, and may be established quickly: in a discussion of Rémy de Gourmont, with whom he contrasts Henry James, Pound writes:

> The mind of Rémy de Gourmont was less like the mind of Henry James than any contemporary mind I can think of. James' drawings of *moeurs contemporaines* was [sic] so circumstantial, so concerned with the setting, with detail, nuance, social aroma, that his transcripts were "out of date" almost before his books had gone into a second edition. . . .
>   In contradiction to, in wholly antipodal distinction from, Henry James, Gourmont was an artist of the nude. He was an intelligence almost more than an artist; when he portrays, he is concerned with hardly more than the permanent human elements. *His people are only by accident of any particular era.*

While the *Cantos* are "a poem including history," Pound's fundamental conception of human existence contains elements that are profoundly anti-historical.[28]

This is perhaps seen most clearly in another context, an essay on Joyce's play *Exiles*, in which Pound writes, "You must remember that all the real problems of life are insoluble." The *real* matter of interest in history cannot then be properly historical, but rather that which stands out against the welter of the merely historical, just as the "live man" Odysseus stands out among "the duds," making him a "subject-rhyme," as Hugh Kenner puts it, with the other heroes of the *Cantos*.[29] Indeed, the typography of "MA QVESTO," as well as the use of Roman numerals in the Fascist calendar, are meant to indicate Mussolini's place in the pantheon of Roman emperors, with the Italian Fascist state seen as a revival of the ancient Roman state, a return to an essentially timeless Roman virtue.

Furthermore, the draining of the swamps not only establishes a humanized, redeemed space where previously confusion reigned, but it also permits the completion of a ritual act that links the practical-technical with the sacred, as illustrated by the line "Waited 2000 years, ate grain from the marshes." For Pound the production of grain is part of a solar religion that

28. Pound, *Literary Essays*, 339–40, 86.
29. Ezra Pound, *Pound/Joyce: The Letters of Ezra Pound to James Joyce, with Pound's Essays on Joyce*, 56; Hugh Kenner, *The Pound Era*, 93.

links human being to natural cycles. There are other instances—in cantos 45 and 97, for example[30]—of Pound ritualizing the production and eating of grain in such a way as to suggest continuity between the profane world of agriculture and eating and the sacred world of divine power.

Pound's use and vision of Mussolini's land-reclamation project contrasts, then, quite sharply with Rukeyser's use and vision of the New River diversion. The differences between Pound and Rukeyser here seem to come down to three. First, Rukeyser presents the hydroelectric project as a complex meeting of the greed of Union Carbide Corporation, the engineering talents of the New Kanawha staff, the ruthlessness of the Rinehart and Dennis Company, and the effort and sacrifice of the men who worked on the project. Thus the project may not ultimately be reduced to the will of a single individual. If the project may be reduced at all from the complexity of these interacting elements, it would be to the mass of workers eulogized in the final poem in the cycle, and not to any single "mastermind." This contrasts with Pound's focus in Canto 41 on Mussolini as the animating will behind the land-reclamation project and, more generally, with one of Pound's fundamental principles for the analysis of history, locating the "factive" ruler, to whose will the proper governance of the state may be entrusted.

Second, Rukeyser sees the hydroelectric project as an event in a history that is linear (a term that is currently considered derogative). That is, while she places the construction of the tunnel and the entire project within the history of the United States and, more locally, of West Virginia, she sees the project as an outcome of this history, and not as the return of a previous historical moment. Rukeyser is committed to a roughly progressive view of history (about which I will have more to say later on) that is fundamentally incompatible with Pound's vision of recurrence.

Third, while Pound's use of mythic and ritual elements links the historical event of the draining of the marshes to the realm of the recurrent, Rukeyser uses these same elements in a more provisional way. In her hands, they provide a way to attempt to imagine the forces of the contemporary world, which otherwise seem so resistant to the imagination. If Pound's vision of a cyclical history articulates the mythic as that which persists even in degenerate eras, Rukeyser's vision of history permits no such thing. Rather, the mythic fulfills in her text a function that might be called ideological, in the neutral sense. Thus the mythic provides a way to

---

30. Canto 45: "with usura, sin against nature, / is thy bread ever more of stale rags / is thy bread dry as paper, / with no mountain wheat, no strong flour" (*Cantos*, 229); Canto 97: "Luigi, *gobbo*, makes his communion with wheat grain / in the hill paths / at sunrise" (693). Robert Casillo discusses this solar religion and its connection to both agrarianism and anti-Semitism in his provocative but flawed *Genealogy of Demons: Anti-Semitism, Fascism, and the Myths of Ezra Pound*, 99–102.

imagine and conceptualize the present in terms that transcend the every-day. Rather than constituting a move *away* from history, myth as Rukeyser uses it moves us away from the mere facticity of the everyday and toward a history into whose meaning we may enquire. In Pound the mythic is intran-sitive, an end in itself, while in Rukeyser it is transitive, leading to the level of the historical. In terms of the vision of the two poets with regard to these fairly similar poetic projects, Pound and Rukeyser are at extreme odds.

It is worth noting that Michael André Bernstein argues persuasively that the characteristics of the *Cantos* that I discuss above were not a product of Pound's direct intention, but rather of the interaction of several objec-tions on Pound's part to organizing his great poem upon "principles of se-quence or chronology." Bernstein holds that Pound's method of drawing upon a chronologically disordered sequence of historical events and fig-ures need not result in the effective abolition of "temporal causality from the domain of historical endeavor." While I largely agree with Bernstein, one of the objections to "principles of sequence or chronology" seems to me to doom the *Cantos* as a properly historical project: "Pound's two prin-cipal and interrelated axes for judging any era . . . the absolute authority of the 'factive' ruler to determine the welfare of his people, and the degree of interest rate tolerated as the key to economic justice." As Bernstein notes, these axes are "radically ahistorical and timeless." Thus they would ap-pear to scuttle from the outset any attempt to deal with history as history. Bernstein seems to sense as much, commenting that they present "in many ways . . . the most troubling of all" of Pound's objections to chronology or sequentiality.[31]

It is tempting to speculate on the degree of connection between Pound's antihistorical criteria for the evaluation of history and his neo-Platonism, insightfully discussed by Bernstein. Neo-Platonism is marked by its hostil-ity to mediation, its desire for the immediacy of experience or meaning. This is especially clear in Plotinus's encomium to Egyptian hieroglyph-ics, quoted by Bernstein. Hegel, the very philosopher of mediation, placed Egyptian culture quite low in his historical/conceptual gradation of art because of this characteristic. Pound's desire for immediacy, famously ex-pressed in his doctrine of the ideogrammatic method, might very well be held responsible for the absence of relations between moments in both his mythical vision and his historical vision. As Bernstein puts it, "The connec-tions between the moment of vision and the surrounding darkness are elab-orated no more clearly in the mythical realm than they are in his chronicle of factual events."[32] Pound's focus on the supposedly eternal within history

---

31. Bernstein, *Tale of the Tribe,* 110–14.
32. Ibid., 92.

and his desire for immediacy thus appear linked, and help to illuminate by way of contrast Rukeyser's emphasis on process and mediation.

Comparisons of Rukeyser with MacLeish, Eliot, and Pound point out that *The Book of the Dead* as a whole, but most specifically "The Cornfield" and the meditative sequence that poem initiates, is marked by its acceptance of the nature of historical time, or, simply, by its acceptance of history as such. Simultaneously, the mythic dimension of *The Book of the Dead* is as pronounced in "The Cornfield" as at any other point in the cycle. The poem's "mythic" concern with resurrection may be reconciled with its seemingly contradictory emphasis on history, because the possibility of resurrection—connected to the project of redeeming, to whatever extent possible, the lives of the dead workers—takes concrete form in the exposure of the wrong done to the workers and the realization of the utopian possibilities that inhere in their lives.

"Alloy," the second poem of the meditative sequence, immediately follows "Arthur Peyton," a proximity that reflects their thematic interconnectedness. "Alloy" almost literally begins where "Arthur Peyton" leaves off, despite the shift in mode from monologue to meditation. Like "Arthur Peyton," the initial stanzas of "Alloy" emphasize the negativity of the tunnel project and its silica byproduct:

> This is the most audacious landscape. The gangster's
> stance with his gun smoking and out is not so
> vicious as this commercial field, its hill of glass.
>
> Sloping as gracefully as thighs, the foothills
> narrow to this, clouds over every town
> finally indicate the stored destruction.
>
> Crystalline hill: a blinded field of white
> murdering snow, seamed by convergent tracks;
> the travelling cranes reach for the silica.   (92)

On one level, much of "Alloy" simply describes the ultimate destination of the silica and the purpose to which it was put. But the "alloy" of the title refers at once to three things: to the town, originally named Boncar, where the steel processing plant was located; to the ferrosilicon alloy produced in the plant; and to the alloy of the negative and the positive produced by *The Book of the Dead*.

Appropriately, "Alloy" is itself an alloy, processing the negativity of "Arthur Peyton" so that it may present the silica extracted from the tunnel as something at least two-sided: the poem alternates between the negative, destructive, murderous quality of the silica and its positive quality as something useful that has been wronged by being made into an instrument of destruction. One can thus see four moments in "Alloy." The first is that expressed in the stanzas quoted above, which carry over the mood of "Arthur Peyton." The second moment is that in stanzas four through six, where the silica enters into the production of steel:

> electric furnaces produce this precious, this clean,
> annealing the crystals, fusing at last alloys.
>
> Hottest for silicon, blast furnaces raise flames,
> spill fire, spill steel, quench the new shape to freeze,
> tempering it to perfected metal.   (92)

Here the silica is physically transformed into ferrosilicon alloy, simultaneously adding to its character as stored destruction the quality of being useful and part of a technological process that is presented as in its own right a thing of beauty. The ambivalence here is heightened by the contrast between the durability of the metal produced and the frailty of the humans who produce it.

This frailty underlies the third moment, in stanzas seven and eight, in which the windblown dust and the smoke rising from the mill serve as reminders of the death and suffering of the tunnel workers exposed to the silica dust, more deadly than the emissions from the steel mill. The eighth stanza reads:

> The roaring flowers of the chimney-stacks
> less poison, at their lips in fire, than this
> dust that is blown from off the field of glass; (92)

The ninth and final stanza presents the fourth moment, in which the silica becomes an ambivalent angel, destructive but useful, deadly but wronged. The dust of the previous stanza

> blows and will blow, rising over the mills,
> crystallized and beyond the fierce corrosion
> disintegrated angel on these hills.   (92)

Both innocent and deadly, Rukeyser's "disintegrated angel" resembles the angels in Rilke's *Duino Elegies,* who are unwittingly attractive and dangerous to mortals. But unlike Rilke's angels, the "disintegrated angel" is a natural substance extracted through labor, rather than a hypothetical supernatural being.

The attitude Rukeyser would have us take to this product of human intervention into nature appears to be close to the attitude that, according to

Susan Buck-Morss, Walter Benjamin would have us take to a downed Luft-waffe plane depicted in a photograph: sadness for the plane itself, whose utopian character as the fulfillment of the agelong dream of flight has been perverted by being harnessed to fascism.[33] Buck-Morss refers to a passage in *The Arcades Project*, in which Benjamin quotes Pierre-Maxime Schuhl: "The bombers remind us of what Leonardo da Vinci expected of man in flight: that he was to ascend to the skies 'in order to seek snow on the mountaintops and bring it back to the city to spread on the sweltering streets in summer.' "[34] Far from apologizing for the uses to which the objects they treat are put, Rukeyser's and Benjamin's utopian refunctioning of technology and its products rebuke a world that can countenance such uses.

Like "Alloy," "Power" is a poem with a very deliberate, if less obvious, structure. It begins on the earth's surface, where the energy of the sun is transferred to the planet, then proceeds downward, through the walkways beneath the power plant that converts the diverted river's force into electric power. This journey, as well as a quotation from *Paradise Lost*, draws attention to the epic—in the conventional sense—quality of *The Book of the Dead*, here seen in the fulfillment of the obligation to descend to and encounter the underworld. The poem begins immersed in the beauty and vitality of the scene, with intricately interlaced grammatical structures, numerous present-participial constructions, and enjambed or only lightly end-stopped lines conveying a sense of a fecund natural world. This nature is found concentrated in the river, "magnificent flower on the mouth" (93), which eventually yields up some of its power to the turbines of the hydroelectric dam.

Also on the surface are the pylons supporting the electrical lines that transport the electricity generated in the plant. In one of the most striking stanzas of the meditative sequence, Rukeyser describes a product of technology in terms appropriate to an anthropomorphized god. Her sense of the beauty and grace inhering in the products of the modern world contrasts with the backward-looking utopianism of Eliot and Pound.

> Steel-bright, light-pointed, the narrow-waisted towers
> lift their protective network, the straight, the accurate
> flex of distinction, economy of gift,

33. Susan Buck-Morss, lecture, Duke University, Durham, N.C., October 28, 1989. The photograph can be found in Buck-Morss's book *The Dialectics of Seeing*, 330. John Dos Passos seems to be indicating something similar in his "biography" of the Wright brothers in *U.S.A.* The wonder of these two bicycle mechanics producing a machine capable of flight is immediately juxtaposed with the horror of the purposes to which their invention is put in the First World War (297).

34. Walter Benjamin, *The Arcades Project*, 486.

gymnast, they poise their freight; god's generosity! give
their voltage low enough for towns to handle.   (93)

The humanization of the technological in this Promethean image both pre-
pares for and contrasts with the technological utopianism of "the engineer
Jones," who will guide the speaker of the poem into the depths.

Jones appears in a stanza in which the power line is figured not as an
anthropomorphized god, but rather as a roadway:

This is the midway between water and flame,
this is the road to take when you think of your country,
between the dam and the furnace, terminal.   (93)

By echoing the "roads" refrain established in the first poem of the cycle
("This is the road"), Rukeyser emphasizes that the scene of the Gauley
Tunnel tragedy is a concentrated version of America. Accordingly, what
follows is, as in the previous poem, an "alloy" of the positive and the neg-
ative, of the utopian and the anti-utopian, of power harnessed to enrich
life and of a different kind of power used to destroy the lives of those who
make that "road" possible. But where the positive element in "Alloy" tends
to inhere in the silica, in "Power" the positive radiates outward from the
human construct of the dam itself. The speaker in the poem is led through
the hydroelectric facility by O. M. Jones, the designer of the project and a
technological utopian:[35]

"They said I built the floor like the tiles of a bank,
I wanted the men who work here to be happy." (93)

But Jones's vision is one-sided indeed; he is, Rukeyser seems to suggest by
having him quote Milton, blind to an entire dimension of the dam's reality
and able to see only the dam's beauty. Further, Jones's comment about the
"Black Hole of Calcutta" places him politically on the opposite side from
Rukeyser; it alludes to an essay that Vito Marcantonio published in the *New
Republic* in which the tunnel shafts are referred to as "modern Black Holes
of Calcutta":[36]

35. O. M. Jones was the chief engineer of New Kanawha Power Company and a
longtime employee of the Electro-Metallurgical Company, one of four companies that
merged in 1917 to form Union Carbide and Carbon Corporation. He supervised the de-
sign of the tunnel and, operating a steam shovel, took the symbolic first shovel of dirt
in the construction of the hydroelectric project (Cherniack, *Hawk's Nest Incident*, 11, 17).
36. Vito Marcantonio, "Dusty Death," 106.

> Go down; here are the outlets, butterfly valves
> open from here, the tail-race, vault of steel,
> the spiral staircase ending, last light in shaft.
> "Gone," says the thin straight man.
> " 'Hail, holy light, offspring of Heav'n first-born,
> 'Or of th' Eternal Coeternal beam
> 'May I express thee unblamed?' "
>
> And still go down.
>
> Now ladder-mouth; and the precipitous fear,
> uncertain rungs down into after-night.
> "This is the place. Away from this my life
> I am indeed Adam unparadiz'd.
> Some fools call this the Black Hole of Calcutta,
> I don't know how they ever get to Congress."   (94)

The physical journey into the mountain's interior, shepherded by this man who sees only beauty in the hydroelectric project, is a journey into a literal darkness, but also a figurative journey into the night of the man's skewed vision. Rukeyser balances the utopian vision of a technology made congenial to humanity in the "narrow-waisted towers" with the technological utopianism of Jones, who cannot see the horror that lies behind the project in which he takes such pride.

Serving as an unwitting Virgil, Jones guides the speaker and the reader into the inferno of the power plant's underworld, with the tone of the poem becoming increasingly dark as the journey descends ever deeper. The completion of the journey from the surface into the depths leads to a moment that rivals the negativity of "Arthur Peyton," as the power generated by the dam appears in the aspect of death:

> Down the reverberate channels of the hills
> the suns declare midnight, go down, cannot ascend,
> no ladder back; see this, your eyes can ride through steel,
> this is the river Death, diversion of power,
> the root of the tower and the tunnel's core,
> this is the end.   (95)

Rukeyser, for all her appreciation of the beauty of the project, both in the abstract (as power harnessed to fill human needs) and the concrete (the grace of an electrical pylon), sees the one-sided celebration of this beauty as an essentially infernal vision.

Following immediately upon "Power," "The Dam" is arguably the most powerful of this group of three poems, which, in their meditative quality, resemble the later poetry of Wallace Stevens. While the meditative section of *The Book of the Dead* tends more toward the abstract and the collective than do the concrete and personal monologues such as "Mearl Blankenship" and "Absalom," even here Rukeyser does not abandon her previous procedures. "The Dam" is punctuated by documentary and mythical incursions. In "The Dam," as elsewhere, Rukeyser sets herself the task of keeping in play both the positive and negative aspects of the tunnel project. The dominant mood of the poem is more or less contemplative, processing the fact of the dam and the power generated by it through a consideration of the flux of the water that yields its energy to the dam's turbines. In this way Rukeyser converts the negativity of "Power" into something positive. This transformation shifts the poem's focus to a central concern of Rukeyser, one that provides for her, as for Ernst Bloch, the ground of hope in even the worst of circumstances: process. In "The Dam," Rukeyser transforms the negativity of the previous poem's terminus into a source of hope.

Whereas the conclusion of "Power" forces us to acknowledge the irreducible fact of the deaths that underlie the hydroelectric complex, "The Dam" brings us out of those infernal depths and permits us to glimpse another, greater, reality, that of transformation and energy. Thus these two poems stand in a relation to each other not unlike that of the *Inferno* and the *Purgatorio*, since the crucial difference between them is the difference between Hell, which forms a pure terminus—duration without the possibility of change—and Purgatory, which, while not pleasant, offers that which must be abandoned when one enters the infernal region: hope, which is sustained through change.

Rukeyser alerts the reader to the relationship between "The Dam" and the previous poem in the first line: "All power is saved, having no end" (95). The terminus of the previous poem is, from the perspective of this poem, only an appearance. The river of death of the previous poem is also the river whose

> Water celebrates, yielding continually
> sheeted and fast in its overfall
> slips down the rock, evades the pillars
> building its colonnades, repairs
> in stream and standing wave
> retains its seaward green
> broken by obstacle rock; falling, the water sheet
> spouts, and the mind dances, excess of white.
> White brilliant function of the land's disease. (95)

Rukeyser reinforces the theme of this stanza by combining the enjambment of all lines until the penultimate with frequent caesuras, suggesting the interrupted but unstoppable energy of the water running its course.

This energy is not violated, Rukeyser emphasizes in the next stanza, by being partially harnessed:

> Many-spanned, lighted, the crest leans under
> concrete arches and the channelled hills,
> turns in the gorge toward its release;
> kinetic and controlled, the sluice
> urging the hollow, the thunder,
> the major climax
>   energy
> total and open watercourse
> praising the spillway, fiery glaze,
> crackle of light, cleanest velocity
> flooding, the moulded force.   (95)

The phrase "moulded force" combines the fluid dynamism of the water and the immovability of the solid rock and concrete. This relation is so basic that it cannot be violated by human intervention in the process. (Rukeyser might at this point be seen to offer a physical counterpart to the biological in Williams's "Spring and All.") Indeed—and this is crucial to and characteristic of Rukeyser—part of the beauty and significance of what was built in and around Gauley Mountain derives precisely from human intervention in physical processes at a point that is fundamental and, loosely speaking, mysterious, such as that at which water, in a sense, becomes electricity and light.

But Rukeyser does not remain within the philosophical and the mythological in "The Dam." As in *The Book of the Dead* as a whole, she plays the more exalted language and concerns of the poem off of the reality of the conditions under which the work was done.

> They poured the concrete and the columns stood,
> laid bare the bedrock, set the cells of steel,
> a dam for monument was what they hammered home.
> Blasted, and stocks went up;
> insured the base,
> and limousines
> wrote their own graphs upon
> roadbed and lifeline.   (96–97)

Like John Brown, those who built the dam are memorialized by a monument, although theirs is of their own making. And like Brown, many of them have died in an unequal struggle that Rukeyser would have us remember still continues. Rukeyser now shifts to the terms in which this struggle was played out, but before she does so, she reminds the reader,

"Their hands touched mastery" (97). Perhaps more clearly here than any-where else in the entire cycle, those who worked on the dam are positioned between realities: on the one hand, they "insured the base," as Rukeyser, making a sardonic Marxist joke, puts it; and on the other, they "touched mastery," entering into the realm of elementary physical forces and touch-ing the possibility of human mastery of the conditions of existence, the possibility of real human freedom. They are simultaneously victims and heroes.

In the next stanza, though, Rukeyser reduces the dam project to its crud-est terms: it is "a racket" presided over by the corporate analogues to "ordinary machine gun racketeers" (97), she writes, quoting heavily from the transcript of the House subcommittee hearing. Drawing quotations from scattered portions of the testimony and questioning, she presents the project in the worst possible light in order to offer the strongest contrast with its aspect of "mastery" and even with the negative but elevated sense of the project as infernal. Here Rukeyser presents that aspect of the project in which it is neither masterful nor infernal, but merely criminal:

> Mr. Dunn. When they were caught at it they resorted to the methods
>   employed by gunmen, ordinary machine gun racketeers. They cowardly
>   tried to buy out the people who had the information on them.
> . . . .
> Miss Allen. Mr. Jesse J. Ricks, the president of the Union Carbide & Carbon
>   Corporation, suggested that the stockholder had better take this question
>   up in a private conference.
> The dam is safe. A scene of power.
> The dam is the father of the tunnel.
> This is the valley's work, the white, the shining.

		Stock and Dividend in Dollars					Net	Closing		
High	Low		Open	High	Low	Last	Chge.	Bid	Ask	Sales
111	61¼	Union Carbide (3.20)	67¼	69½	67¼	69½	+3	69¼	69½	3,400

(97)

Rukeyser identifies Union Carbide unambiguously as the efficient, if not the final, cause of the tragedy by reproducing the stock report. In addi-tion, as Michael Thurston notes, the stock market quotation "literally em-bodies blockage," the blockage of the victims' lungs, of the investigation of the tragedy, of adequate legislation to protect workers; "[s]et off from the surrounding text by solid horizontal lines, it cuts the page in half."[37] But Rukeyser also implicates the entire capitalist system that generates this

37. Thurston, "Documentary Modernism," 77.

form of reporting and by virtue of which Union Carbide exists, as she re-
duces the hydroelectric project to its lowest and most derogatory terms.

Because that project has just been characterized so derisively, the final
stanza is all the more stunning. The workers, now generalized as the largely
anonymous masses who have done the world's work throughout human
history, are likened to the pure and indefatigable energy of water:

> This is a perfect fluid, having no age nor hours,
> surviving scarless, unaltered, loving rest,
> willing to run forever to find its peace
> in equal seas in currents of still glass.
> Effects of friction : to fight and pass again,
> learning its power, conquering boundaries,
> able to rise blind in revolts of tide,
> broken and sacrificed to flow resumed.
> Collecting eternally power. Spender of power,
> torn, never can be killed, speeded in filaments,
> million, its power can rest and rise forever,
> wait and be flexible. Be born again.
> Nothing is lost, even among the wars,
> imperfect flow, confusion of force.
> It will rise. These are the phases of its face.
> It knows its seasons, the waiting, the sudden.
> It changes. It does not die.   (97–98)

This conclusion features dramatically uneven rhythm and tempo. It alter-
nates rapid and slow movement, interrupted by pauses but also speed-
ing along at times, and plays mono- and polysyllabism both with and
against the grain of other elements. Rukeyser attempts to present ono-
matopoeically the very course of history in a poem dedicated to disclosing
its movement, which is characterized by pain ("blind," "broken," "sac-
rificed," "torn") but also by the struggle and the tendency toward over-
throwing "all those conditions in which man is an abased, enslaved, aban-
doned, contemptible being," as Marx so memorably put it.[38]

By equal turns Whitmanesque and Marxist, "The Dam" synthesizes the
polar roles that Rukeyser assigns to the workers, those of victims and
heroes. The workers on the Gauley Tunnel project here join the greater col-
lectivity of the working class and become a part of its history. The deaths of
the tunnel workers are inserted into a narrative of human emancipation in
which the working class, suffering greatly along the way, makes possible
for the first time real human freedom. *The Book of the Dead* earns the great

38. Karl Marx, "Contribution to the Critique of Hegel's *Philosophy of Right:* Introduc-
tion," 60.

hope expressed in "The Dam" by its passage through the most infernal and criminal depths—by confronting the real opposite of emancipation that was the fate of the tunnel workers—before emerging, here, into the light. Where "Absalom" achieved a reconciliation of subject and object, of death and possibility, on the ground of the concretely singular, the individual, and the personal, "The Dam" does so on the ground of the more generally historical and collective.

Taken as a whole, the meditative series of poems presents an argument about history and the place in it of the great majority of humankind whose labor makes human life possible. In a sense, the argumentative character of these poems is quite similar to that found in a poet such as Stevens, in whose work a contention between two concepts is often the structuring principle. Rukeyser similarly builds these meditative poems around a framework of argument, with the difference that where Stevens presents conflicts between abstract concepts—reality and imagination—locked in static opposition to each other, Rukeyser is concerned with conflicts between the tendential forces (themselves of course abstractions, though at a different level) operative in history, forces whose relations are dynamic, which imparts to her poems a dialectical quality similar to that found in the famous brief résumé of history in the first section of *The Communist Manifesto.*

Coda: "The Book of the Dead"

The eponymous conclusion of *The Book of the Dead* places the poem's subject in the context of both an American and a more global history. Written in a controlled, relatively formal style and in three-line, unrhymed stanzas, the final poem makes forays into other poetic and other discursive modes: the catechism, the prospect poem, and the public poem in the tradition of the American jeremiad. Contributing to the sense of formality and closure is the return of the "road" refrain in the first line of the poem: "These roads will take you into your own country" (102).

"The Book of the Dead" comprises three distinct sections separated by ruled lines; in the first of these, Rukeyser surveys American history. She gestures toward the prospect poem and public poetry such as that written in the nineteenth century by James Russell Lowell and others:

> The facts of war forged into actual grace.
> Seasons and modern glory.   Told in the histories,
>   how first ships came

> seeing on the Atlantic thirteen clouds
> lining the west horizon with their white
> shining halations;
>
> they conquered, throwing off impossible Europe— (102)

Rukeyser appears to be invoking the precedent of a poem such as Lowell's "An Ode. For the Fourth of July, 1876":

> Seven years long was the bow
> Of battle bent, and the heightening
> Storm-heaps convulsed with the throe
> Of their uncontainable lightning;
> Seven years long heard the sea
> Crash of navies and wave-borne thunder;
> Then drifted the cloud-rack a-lee,
> And new stars were seen, a world's wonder;
> Each by her sisters made bright,
> All binding all to their stations,
> Cluster of manifold light
> Startling the old constellations.

Both Lowell and Rukeyser invoke the American past as part of a critical project, though from rather different perspectives. Lowell follows the tradition of the American jeremiad, setting up a straightforward contrast between a noble past and a fallen present:

> Murmur of many voices in the air
> Denounces us degenerate,
> Unfaithful guardians of a noble fate.[39]

Rukeyser presents the advent of the United States in a generally—though far from exclusively—positive manner, though one that is less rhetorically strained than that of Lowell.

For Rukeyser, the story of the United States may be regarded positively insofar as it is part of the story of humanity attempting to wrest control of history:

> Before our face the broad and concrete west,
> green ripened field, frontier pushed back like river
> controlled and dammed;   (103)

39. Harry Hayden Clark and Norman Foerster, eds., *James Russell Lowell: Representative Selections*, 211–21, lines 53–64, 195–97.

As with her understanding of the damming of the river, so too within Rukeyser's history of America there is a profound ambivalence. This foray into American history begins with "The facts of war," including the war fought between those who built the Gauley Tunnel and those who profited from their labor: a war of class against class, a war internal to America, unlike Lowell's romanticized, decidedly nineteenth-century version of the American Revolution. Furthermore, Rukeyser's Europe, unlike that of the American jeremiad, is not only the moribund and corrupt Old World ("impossible Europe"), but also a place that sends "new signals from the hero hills / near Barcelona" (103), the signals of the Spanish Civil War and of a people determined (though tragically unable, as it turned out) to forge their own future.

Given these qualifications, which reveal the critical nature of Rukeyser's engagement with the traditional public poem about America, the first section of "The Book of the Dead" fittingly concludes with considerably more ambivalence than does Lowell's poem. The United States presents itself as

> sums of frontiers
>
> and unmade boundaries of acts and poems,
> the brilliant scene between the seas, and standing,
>   this fact and this disease.   (103)

The logic of the poem does not permit the easy disavowal of Lowell's jeremiad, in which the possibility that the seeds of present trouble lie in the hallowed past is never acknowledged. By ending the section with "disease," by exploiting the word's rhyme with "the seas," and by the use of "brilliant," which in *The Book of the Dead* usually describes the combined beauty and deadliness of silica, Rukeyser sets up a rather different relationship than does Lowell between that of which she approves and that of which she is critical. The net effect is embodied in a catalogue of American scenes that offers exhilarating vistas: "the flashing wheatfields, cities," as well as their opposites, "lunar plains / grey in Nevada" (103). The sense of liberation and promise in the poem rebukes the horror of "this fact and this disease," yet without unduly idealizing that world of which the Gauley Tunnel tragedy is one terrible manifestation. "The Book of the Dead" thus develops through a contrapuntal movement brought to completion only in the poem's conclusion.

The second section has a curious structure: it falls into two groups of three stanzas each, followed by a four-stanza group. The first two groups each consist of two stanzas concerned with the realm of myth followed by a contrasting stanza concerned with the here-and-now of the New River valley. The first group contrasts a dimly lit world of mythic consciousness with the clarity and urgency of the present and the near:

> Half-memories absorb us, and our ritual world
> carries its history in familiar eyes,
> planted in flesh it signifies its music
>
> in minds which turn to sleep and memory,
> in music knowing all the shimmering names,
> the spear, the castle, and the rose.
>
> But planted in our flesh these valleys stand,
> everywhere we begin to know the illness,
> are forced up, and our times confirm us all. (103–4)

Clearly alluding to *The Waste Land*, these lines reprise briefly—though not for the last time—the critique of modernist mythmaking found in "The Cornfield."

The second group contrasts with the first in that where the first offers only the dim light of "half-memories," the second presents "a fertilizing image," that of a "Carthaginian" goddess (a version of Isis?), "a tall woman" who

> carries in her two hands the book and cradled dove,
> on her two thighs, wings folded from the waist
> cross to her feet, a pointed human crown.   (104)

This "fertilizing image" provides a positive counterpoint to the death and destruction the poem has surveyed, as well as to the apparent infertility of "the spear, the castle, and the rose." Following the description of the goddess figure, the poem breaks into a present with which this "fertilizing image" also contrasts:

> This valley is given to us like a glory.
> To friends in the old world, and their lifting hands
> that call for intercession. Blow falling full in face. (104)

Again, presumably, Rukeyser is alluding to Spain and the failure of the United States and other nominally democratic nations to respond to the attack on the Spanish Republic. The failure of the United States to live up to its best tradition is manifested by its indifference and even active hostility to the Republic, just as it is manifested by the fate of the tunnel workers.

The section concludes with a four-stanza group that issues a call to reengage the world of the present, an extended summons reminiscent of the end of *Song of Myself* in the directness of its address and in its anticipation of affecting the reader:

All those whose childhood made learn skill to meet,
and art to see after the change of heart;
all the belligerents who know the world.

You standing over gorges, surveyors and planners,
you workers and hope of countries, first among powers;
you who give peace and bodily repose,

opening landscapes by grace, giving the marvel lowlands
physical peace, flooding old battlefields
with general brilliance, who best love your lives;

and you young, you who finishing the poem
wish new perfection and begin to make;
you men of fact, measure our times again.   (104)

In a final critical engagement with her mythically minded contemporaries, Rukeyser not only juxtaposes her poem with the "half-memory" of "the spear, the castle, and the rose," but also alludes to the direct address in the "Death by Water" section of *The Waste Land*:

> Gentile or Jew
> O you who turn the wheel and look to windward,
> Consider Phlebas, who was once handsome and tall as you. (lines 319–21)

Whereas Eliot's memento mori turns the reader's eye to eternity (though this, like most statements about *The Waste Land*, is arguable), Rukeyser's direct address returns the reader to the things of this world, to the forces and processes that shape the future.

Having taken the measure—in the double sense of having put in measures and having assessed—of her times, Rukeyser concludes "The Book of the Dead" with a synthetic fifteen-stanza coda that reprises the major themes and motifs of the entire cycle. She begins with an affirmation of the working class:

These are our strength, who strike against history.
Those whose corrupt cells owe their new styles of weakness
            to our diseases;   (104)

She goes on to list some of the horrors to which the workers of the world are subject. But, as elsewhere in the cycle, these people are both victims and heroes; they have allies and, vulnerable to destruction at every turn, are given voice by this poem that recognizes the danger but also the tendency of humanity to seek to liberate itself to the greatest degree possible from the realm of necessity.

These stanzas move forward urgently, with the mixture of enjambed and end-stopped lines, and of lines with and without caesuras, generating a rhythm of rapid advance and brief, clarifying pauses. The section reaches its rhythmic as well as conceptual climax in the final three stanzas:

> Down coasts of taken countries, mastery,
> discovery at one hand, and at the other
>   frontiers and forests,
>
> fanatic cruel legend at our back and
> speeding ahead the red and open west,
>   and this our region,
>
> desire, field, beginning. Name and road,
> communication to these many men,
> as epilogue, seeds of unending love. (105)

Rukeyser condenses the greater part of her long poem into a few lines here. The "red and open west" both spatializes history (just as folk culture often presents distance in time as distance in space) and politicizes it, projecting a "red," presumably classless, future. This future is the ultimate ground of the poem, the projected temporal place in light of which the poem has been written and must be read: it is "our region," the home we have never had and to which we must turn. The reader moves ahead, located between past and future, between the "fanatic cruel legend at our back and / speeding ahead the red and open west." The utopian dimension of the poem here presents itself explicitly as the goal of the cycle's movement, undergirding its role as the normative standpoint from which the cycle's judgments have been made and upon which its aesthetic is based.

In this penultimate stanza, Rukeyser presents a figure to compete with Walter Benjamin's famed angel of history in the ninth of his "Theses on the Philosophy of History":

> His face is turned toward the past. Where we perceive a chain of events, he sees one single catastrophe which keeps piling wreckage upon wreckage and hurls it in front of his feet. The angel would like to stay, awaken the dead, and make whole what has been smashed. But a storm is blowing from Paradise; it has got caught in his wings with such violence that the angel can no longer close them. This storm irresistibly propels him into the future to which his back is turned, while the pile of debris before him grows skyward. This storm is what we call progress.[40]

While Benjamin's thesis is open to interpretation—his parabolic style sees to this—it is clearly directed in part against the confidence in the future

---

40. Walter Benjamin, "Theses on the Philosophy of History," 258.

held by Marxists of the social democratic variety. Progress, in both this particular thesis and in Benjamin's work generally, is distrusted insofar as it rests on a vision of an inexorable, mild stream of steady improvement. Benjamin's vision—true to that of Marx in this regard—is rather one of progress by catastrophe.

This vision clearly accords with Rukeyser's in *The Book of the Dead*. Yet Rukeyser's vision, so close to Benjamin's, is decidedly different in tone and emphasis. For whereas the angel of history gazes back upon a past it is powerless to affect, Rukeyser's reader is invited to look out upon an "open" future. Benjamin's vision is relentlessly backward-looking, though in a manner different from that which is usually meant by this expression. Benjamin's backward-looking gaze does not rest upon past greatness, but upon past horror; indeed, it is part of his critique of the conventional writing of history that its perspective is typically that of the victors.[41] Rukeyser's vision, while it casts more than a fleeting glance backward, projects forward.

Thus, rather than Benjamin it is again Ernst Bloch, among the figures in the Marxist pantheon, to whom Rukeyser is closest. Like Bloch, Rukeyser maintains a stance that is both future-oriented and capable of a meaningful engagement with the past. As Ze'ev Levy points out:

> Although Bloch's thought focuses on the "final goal," he does not neglect the role of the "primordial cause." It also has its proper place in his concept of utopia. It is motivated by a more or less hidden cosmic drive which Bloch designates as "hunger."[42]

While the structure of Benjamin's thought relies upon a (perhaps figurative) Paradise away from which the storm of progress blows the angel of history,[43] there is no primordial unity in human history for Bloch, nor would there seem to be for Rukeyser.

41. Elsewhere in "Theses on the Philosophy of History," Benjamin writes that to "historians who wish to relive an era, Fustel de Coulanges recommends that they blot out everything that they know about the later course of history. There is no better way of characterizing the method with which historical materialism has broken. It is a process of empathy whose origin is in the indolence of the heart, *acedia*, which despairs of grasping and holding the genuine historical image as it flares up briefly. Among medieval theologians it was regarded as the root cause of sadness. Flaubert, who was familiar with it, wrote 'Peu de gens devineront combien il a fallu être triste pour ressusciter Carthage' [Few will be able to guess how sad one had to be in order to resuscitate Carthage]. The nature of this sadness stands out more clearly if one asks with whom the adherents of historicism actually empathize. The answer is inevitable: with the victor" (256).

42. Ze'ev Levy, "Utopia and Reality in the Philosophy of Ernst Bloch," 176.

43. This is the ineluctable conclusion of Irving Wohlfarth's reading of Benjamin's "Theses." Wohlfarth understands Benjamin as a "triadic thinker," employing the pattern thesis-antithesis-synthesis in the form of a first phase of original unity (Paradise),

More fully than Benjamin's, then, Bloch's pattern accords with Rukeyser's vision in *The Book of the Dead,* a vision rigorously historical as opposed to mythical, so long as "mythical" means "recurrent." Rukeyser's America begins not in a state of unity, not as a Paradise to which we must in some way return (the pattern of both the American jeremiad as well as, by implication, Benjamin's thesis), but rather as a place already in a state of disunion, the place of "the Indian Perecute / and an unnamed indentured English servant" as well as of the explorers Batts, Fallam, and Wood (72). This fundamental incompleteness of the past, this sense of its deficiency, is characteristic not only of Bloch's but of Marx's vision as well, which is, as Jeffrey Vogel cogently puts it, "radically future-oriented."[44] The key lines "fanatic cruel legend at our back and / speeding ahead the red and open west, / and this our region" reveal just how closely Rukeyser's broad view accords with that of Bloch and of the Marxist tradition generally.

Out of a deficient past and moving into a future faced and confronted with hope, *The Book of the Dead* is offered by Rukeyser as "communication to these many men, / as epilogue, seeds of unending love." These lines complete the mythical cycle the poem creates, as the figure of Isis, who gathered the limbs of her beloved Osiris, merges with the mother of "Absalom" and the son of "The Disease: After-Effects"; in these poems, the love between the poetic speaker and a victim of silicosis is the emotional core. It also returns us to the motif of "The Cornfield" in the line "Sowing is over, harvest is coming ripe" (90), with its emphasis on the revolutionary potential latent in historical process.

But here the "seeds of unending love" are a gift to the dead, a gift of love that is not so much unrequited as unrequitable. Love may seem an odd gift to give to these unknown men, but understood properly—that is, not as romantic love—it may be all that can be given. For the utopian projection intricately woven into *The Book of the Dead* cannot itself redeem the dead, as could a supernatural, religious redemption capable of literally overcoming death itself. Were the dead to choose, they would almost certainly choose not to have sacrificed themselves for our future good. Because they gave a gift that must go unreciprocated, *love* is likely the best term we have for that which must be given in return.

---

a second phase of fragmentation, and a third phase of achieved reunification ("On the Messianic Structure of Walter Benjamin's Last Reflections"). Bloch, however, is not a thinker of this kind: he begins with no primordial unity, but rather with a primordial privation, or lack. While the attempt to escape this privation—and achieve "mastery"— is indeed the motor of history, it is a strangely negative form of determination. As Bloch is at pains to explain throughout his work, humanity is also decisively determined by the future, as that against which we prepare and toward which we strive.

44. Jeffrey Vogel, "The Tragedy of History," 45.

Furthermore, "love" returns the longer poem from the climax of "The Dam" to something more modest and moderate, which Rukeyser must do if she is to end the cycle in a manner that comprehends its complex whole. As Staiger notes, while lyric is dominated by "soul," by mood, emotion, and state of mind, drama is dominated by "spirit," or will. As a result, lyric is warm, though ineffectual, and drama cold, though powerful: "Spirit is cold. Whatever reveals spirit and not also soul, spreads light but not warmth. The spirit's achievement is admired. The enchantment of the soul is loved."[45] This feature of the basic components of poetic discourse explains the function of "The Book of the Dead" (which includes the completion of the motif of planting and rebirth) and especially its conclusion. Rukeyser carried multiple burdens in the construction of *The Book of the Dead*. In addition to the various difficulties attendant upon the writing of an ambitious long poem, she faced two burdens specific to the subject she chose: first, to present the facts of the Gauley Tunnel tragedy, and second, to explore the meaning of those facts.

Presenting the facts is the task of the documentary sections of the poem. Exploring the meaning of those facts is the task of both the monologues and the meditative poems. The monologues explore the meaning of the tragedy in its subjective aspect, on the level of the individual; their register is that of "soul." The meditative poems explore the meaning of the tragedy in its historical aspect, on the level of the collective; their register is that of "spirit." Since *The Book of the Dead* aspires to be a work of both soul and spirit, of feeling, fact, and will, Rukeyser needs the final poem to sound each register one last time, to recapitulate the whole which has been painstakingly constructed. She ends with a term of soul, "love," so that as our eyes look to "the red and open west, / and this our region," the vision does not become cold, a mere spirited forgetfulness.

45. Staiger, *Basic Concepts of Poetics*, 182.

5

The Critical Reception
of *The Book of the Dead*

While, as shall become apparent, it oversimplifies matters to divide the response to *The Book of the Dead* into the categories of "negative" and "positive," such a categorization is initially useful. *U.S. 1*, the volume in which *The Book of the Dead* appeared, was widely reviewed upon publication. Responses to *The Book of the Dead* ranged from embarrassment to enthusiasm. This range of reactions gives some insight into the demands made upon Rukeyser as a poet and into the expectations that her critical readers brought to *The Book of the Dead*, expectations that helped or hindered their perception of what I have argued was the nature of her project and her accomplishment.

Negative responses to *The Book of the Dead* typically concentrated upon Rukeyser's heavy use of documentary records. Even those reviewers who clearly admired certain features of Rukeyser's poetry objected to what they saw as the unjustifiably prosaic quality of long sections of the poem. Writing in *Poetry*, Willard Maas, a radical poet and member of the Communist party, conceded: "One admires Miss Rukeyser's inventiveness in . . . *Book of the Dead;* and one admires also her intentions, which are ambitious to the point of audacity." Yet, he said, she strayed "into fields that have been more adequately explored and more tersely recorded by journalists." Maas preferred another section of *U.S. 1* entitled *Night-Music,* a collection of short lyrical poems that Maas characterized as "more subjective" than those of *The Book of the Dead*, which he complained were "modeled after leaflets."[1]

---

1. Willard Maas, "Lost between Wars," 101–2. Maas was careful to point out that there is nothing wrong with leaflets as such: "Not that leaflet writing does not call for an ability of no small proportions; but leaflet writing, as well as poetry trying for the same effect, would appear to be an immediate and transitory art as opposed to one which aims for permanence" (102). See the extended discussion of Maas in Filreis, *Modernism from Right to Left*, 123–34.

Maas's evaluation was shared by another poet-critic closely associated with the Communist party, Eda Lou Walton. Writing in the *New York Times Book Review,* Walton noted that while Rukeyser had attacked some of the problems—in diction, syntax, imagery, and rhythm—of her first volume, *Theory of Flight,* she had reacted too strongly to critics who accused her of being overly subjective and romantic. As a result, in parts of *U.S. 1* she had "made whole groups of poems very prosaic." Walton focused on *The Book of the Dead,* which she characterized as "a report on a village dying of silicosis." The hydroelectric project and the tragedy associated with it, she said, "is the material for poetry, but it is not poetry. This is reporting and not the imaginative vision." Speaking more generally about Rukeyser, Walton offered that her "poetry is uneven because she . . . is trying to grasp a new scene and communicate new reactions to it. She must fuse the personal and the social always. . . . Sometimes, she is too prosaic, sometimes, she is too subjective." Her most successful attempts at the required fusion, according to Walton, came in the best lyrical poems in the *Night-Music* section.[2] Like Maas, Walton qualified her objections to *The Book of the Dead* with praise for Rukeyser's more general project as well as for some of her lyric poems.

Standing between the negative and the positive responses to *The Book of the Dead* were Kerker Quinn and David Wolff. Quinn's review in *New York Herald-Tribune Books* appears to praise and blame the same aspects of the poem. First Quinn favorably contrasts Rukeyser with other young contemporary poets:

> Where her confreres tend to grasp only broad social phenomena, or only iso-lated examples, she captures both the general meaning and the specific detail, plays one against the other, thereby reaching a truer, more moving analysis. Thus, in a series of poems on the death of West Virginia tunnel workmen, whose lungs were needlessly exposed to silica dust, she presents the tragedy from many points of view—through monologues of stricken workmen and members of their families; through testimony of investigating physicians, government committees and sociologists; through graphic accounts of the people's daily life and environment; through meditations on the social issues involved; through stern indictments of the inhumanity which this disaster symbolizes.

In this assessment of Rukeyser, *The Book of the Dead* is used to provide an example of the poet's superior ability and power in relation to her contemporaries, which contrasts with Quinn's treatment of the poem two paragraphs below:

> While it contains some brilliant journalism, and sections of it (The Face of the Dam, Alloy, The Book of the Dead) are poetry of a high order, the sequence

2. Eda Lou Walton, "Muriel Rukeyser's Poems," 19.

is a bit drawn-out, overfreighted with document (despite the ingenuity in molding it to the medium), and lacking in the cumulative power we expect in a work of such length.[3]

Quinn, like Maas and Walton, found the poem excessively journalistic. Like Maas and Walton, he preferred the lyrics of *Night-Music,* as well as the two other long poems, "The Cruise" and "Mediterranean," that come at the end of *U.S. 1.* Yet it is difficult to see how the features of *The Book of the Dead* that Quinn admired could have been attained without some element of the prosaic entering the poem.

Similarly, David Wolff's review in *New Masses*—the lead review in the issue—seems at odds with itself, as if the author was not quite sure what he thought about *The Book of the Dead,* though he did know how he responded to it. Like most reviewers, Wolff emphasized the role of factual documentation in the poem:

> Miss Rukeyser desired to utilize the records of questions and answers, discovering the extraordinary movement of factual document, which proceeds almost dully, then turns and strikes at you with the abrupt violence of the event itself. Documents, skillfully cut, do have a poetic force. But the poet has made an error, this reviewer feels, in not marking off the documents clearly from the body of the poem. Instead, they are divided into lines as if they were poetry—badly phrased poetry, for their internal rhythms conflict with the more rapid and pulse-like beat of poetry; or, very often, the poem itself is converted to factual uses.[4]

Wolff, like Quinn, praised and blamed the same aspect of the poem. In the first half of the quotation above, Wolff characterizes in positive terms his reaction to the contrast between the objective-documentary and subjective-lyrical modes in the poem. The second half rejects the technique that produced this reaction, preferring a separation of prose ("documents") and poetry to Rukeyser's juxtaposition of the epical and lyrical modes of poetry.

Curiously, Wolff went on to praise the "monumentality" of "the conception as a whole"[5]—a monumentality that, one could argue, Rukeyser attained by exploiting the resources of the various poetic modes so adroitly. While the epical mode does not—and, if we accept the traditional view of the matter, should not—attain the intensity of the lyrical, it imparts seriousness and dignity to the subject. The epical dimension of the poem not only provides an objective counterbalance to the subjectivity of the lyrical, it also makes an implicit argument about the "monumentality" of the matter being discussed.

3. Kerker Quinn, "A Modern Poetic Realist," 12.
4. David Wolff, "Document and Poetry," 23–24.
5. Ibid., 23.

Wolff's strictures contrast with the generosity of William Carlos Williams in the *New Republic*. Speaking of *U.S. 1*, Williams, with characteristic indulgence for those whom he felt were innovative and serious, wrote:

> There are moments in the book that are pretty dull, but that's bound to be the character of all good things if they are serious enough: when a devoted and determined person sets out to do a thing he isn't thinking first of being brilliant, he wants to get there even if he has to crawl—on his face. When he is able to—whenever he is able to—he gets up and runs.[6]

Williams's evaluation differs from that of Maas, Walton, Quinn, and Wolff not so much in general terms—he too found the poetry uneven, despite his praise for the book as a whole—as in specifics.

Williams found the strength of *U.S. 1* to lie in the documentary aspect of *The Book of the Dead* as well as in the lyrics of *Night-Music*. The contrast between the positions taken by Rukeyser's other reviewers and Williams is striking. In *The Book of the Dead*, Williams wrote, Rukeyser's

> material, *not* her subject matter but her poetic material, is in part the notes of a congressional investigation, an x-ray report and the testimony of a physician under cross-examination. These she uses with something of the skill employed by Pound in the material of his "Cantos." She knows how to use the *language* of an x-ray report or a stenographic record of a cross-examination. She knows, in other words, how to select and exhibit her material. She understands what words are for and how important it is not to twist them in order to make "poetry" of them.[7]

Explicitly linking Rukeyser's documentary poetics to those of Pound, Williams values precisely that which Rukeyser's other critics disparage, and the use of quotation marks around the word *poetry* has the similar effect of praising Rukeyser where others blame. Williams's generosity is ultimately more precise than the other reviewers' illiberality, since it permits Williams to come to terms with at least part of the method of Rukeyser's poem.

Though he attended more to the general than to the specific, Philip Blair Rice also thought *The Book of the Dead* compelled the attention of the reader. Indeed, after a few comments about *U.S. 1* as a whole (and an offhand dismissal of "The Cruise"), Rice devoted the rest of his *Nation* review to *The Book of the Dead*. Contrasting sharply with Maas, Walton, and Quinn, Rice wrote that *The Book of the Dead* "has the virtues of honest documentary writing, yet keys them to a higher pitch." Like Williams, Rice respected Rukeyser's devotion to the seemingly unpromising reality of Gauley Bridge, her research into the history of West Virginia and the Gauley Tunnel

6. William Carlos Williams, review of *U.S. 1*, 141.
7. Ibid.

tragedy, and her first-person investigation of the scene—all elements that enhance the "prosaic" quality of the poem. Rukeyser's method also drew Rice's praise: "Like a lawyer with an air-tight case, she lets the witnesses tell their own stories, alternating their testimony with the introduction of the written records."[8] Downplaying the role of the lyrical monologues, Rice emphasized the relatively detached way in which Rukeyser presents the tragedy.

Given the combination of her documentary sources and her detached delivery, Rice wrote, Rukeyser's major accomplishment in *The Book of the Dead* lay in the organization of the poem, "the imaginative scheme that holds it together," and it was to this that he turned his attention, concentrating on the role of the Egyptian myth of Osiris. Rice held that the landscape of the Gauley Tunnel tragedy is that of the Egyptian *Book of the Dead:*

> The tunnel is the underworld, the mountain stream is the life-giving river, the Congressional inquiry is the judgment in the Hall of Truth. And the whole tale, of course, is an emblem of rebirth: the dead, in the fullness of time, shall rise to shape a new world. This scheme is suggested rather than presented. Miss Rukeyser has not overweighted her poem with allegory. Yet the few quotations from and allusions to the Egyptian scripture suffice to assimilate the particular incident to a universal pattern, and to give it more than topical significance.[9]

Rice thus shared Williams's opinion of *The Book of the Dead*, but whereas Williams lingered over its documentary character, Rice attended to its lightly worn, but important, mythical superstructure. While I will have occasion to quibble with Rice in the next chapter, he, more than any other contemporary reviewer, perceived the function of the mythical elements of *The Book of the Dead*. I will now look at one more review of *The Book of the Dead*, one that—by omission—provides the term that complements Rice's attention to myth: history.

Writing in *Partisan Review*, Rukeyser's friend John Wheelwright assessed the relative merits of *The Book of the Dead* and *Night-Music* much the same way as did Maas, Walton, and Quinn, though their grounds for assessment differed. Wheelwright, like Maas, Walton, and Williams—indeed, even more so—must be seen as a committed leftist writer.[10] He judged *The Book of the Dead* and *U.S. 1* as a whole by explicitly Marxist standards, as one leftist poet judging a fellow leftist poet. From this perspective he

8. Philip Blair Rice, "The Osiris Way," 335–36.
9. Ibid., 336.
10. While Maas and Walton were associated with the Communist party, Wheelwright was a member first of the Socialist party, which he joined in 1932, and in 1938 a founding member of the Socialist Workers party, which was Trotskyist in orientation and thus vilified by the Communist party (Wald, *Revolutionary Imagination*, 156–61).

felt free to object to what he saw as *The Book of the Dead*'s focus on "the excrescences of capitalism, not the system's inner nature."[11] Because of this misplaced focus, he believed, *The Book of the Dead* becomes an example of muckraking, concentrating upon a particular, isolated incident of a type of abuse that is not intrinsically necessary to the functioning of capitalism as a system.

Wheelwright saw the failure of *The Book of the Dead* to lie in a theoretical or philosophical shortcoming: "A limited philosophy limits poetry; political and aesthetic failings have one root." *The Book of the Dead*, he wrote, is motivated by "unscientific socialism, which shares only in the bourgeois' humanity." The poem thus makes an appeal based on sentiment, failing to indict the system that made the Gauley Tunnel tragedy a piece of rational business practice for Union Carbide. This failure lay behind Rukeyser's extensive attention to nature in the poem. (Presumably Wheelwright had the numerous lines dedicated to the river in mind.) Rather than taking on the artistically challenging task of confronting capitalism and its systematic exploitation of workers—whether they die early of silicosis or not—Rukeyser displaces her, and the reader's, attention onto nature, which presents no great difficulties, available as it is to a traditional romantic repertoire of artistic treatment and audience response. Wheelwright compared Rukeyser to Longfellow, who, in "The Slave in the Dismal Swamp," "knowing less about exploitation than she, was likewise distracted from the difficult human to easy nature."[12] Wheelwright's judgment on *The Book of the Dead* was severe: it is neither good socialism nor good poetry.

Louise Kertesz and Walter Kalaidjian have taken Wheelwright to task for what they see as a fairly brutal mistreatment of Rukeyser. Kertesz disputes the very basis of judgment upon which Wheelwright worked, his assumption that Rukeyser should be judged within the framework of "scientific socialism": " 'The Book of the Dead' is not principally the attack on capitalism reviewers such as John Wheelwright . . . wished she had written." Having thus miscategorized the poem, "[w]hat Wheelwright couldn't see for his limited requirements of poetry was the larger intention and achievement of 'The Book of the Dead,' which is not only political narrative poetry but a poetry which traces the 'immortal necessities' as they have worked in a certain human span in West Virginia."[13] Kertesz's belief that Wheelwright had overly "limited requirements of poetry" springs, apparently, from her illicit identification of Wheelwright's poetics with those of a largely apocryphal "proletarian poetry" of the 1930s. As Alan Wald, Cary Nelson, Alan Filreis, Rita Barnard, and others have shown, the idea that there was a compact, codified, and uniform "proletarian" position in the poetic practices of

11. John Wheelwright, "U.S. 1," 55.
12. Ibid.
13. Kertesz, *Poetic Vision*, 99, 112.

the 1930s is simply false.[14] The widespread desire to produce a revolutionary or proletarian poetry engendered a field of exploration and disputation; Wheelwright's poetics were part of this exploration and disputation. When Wheelwright judged Rukeyser by a single political-aesthetic standard, he judged her within terms that were broadly acceptable to her, however much she might dispute his distinctive poetics or particular verdict.

Like Kertesz, Kalaidjian makes use of Wheelwright's review to show Rukeyser in good light. But where for Kertesz the difference between the two poets is that between a narrow-minded Marxism and a generous humanitarianism, for Kalaidjian the difference is between what he sees as Wheelwright's Marxist, sexist modernism and Rukeyser's (proto-)Foucaultian, feminist postmodernism. According to Kalaidjian, Wheelwright's inability to appreciate *The Book of the Dead* lay in his combined sexism and "classism," both of which were rooted in his Marxism, which mistakenly posited the economic as the "ultimately determining instance," thus instituting the "(male) proletariat class as the privileged bearer of revolution." Such a position, Kalaidjian concludes, rendered Wheelwright unable to perceive the poetics of *The Book of the Dead*, in which Rukeyser "rearticulated the ideological signs of class revolution to a more popular and decidedly feminist discourse."[15]

Unfortunately, Kalaidjian's analysis of Wheelwright's review is vitiated by his misinterpretation of Wheelwright's comment that Rukeyser's poem "attacks the excrescences of capitalism, not the system's inner nature." Kalaidjian, apparently mindful of some of Marx and Engels's comments in *The German Ideology* and of W. J. T. Mitchell's analysis of the same, takes "excrescences" to refer, in classical Marxist fashion, to the ideological emanations of capitalism, in contrast to the more basic functions of the level

14. Wald, *Revolutionary Imagination*; Nelson, *Repression and Recovery*; Filreis, *Modernism from Right to Left*; Barnard, *The Great Depression and the Culture of Abundance: Kenneth Fearing, Nathanael West, and Mass Culture in the 1930s*.

15. Kalaidjian, *American Culture between the Wars*, 164, 163. Michael Thurston also singles out Wheelwright, citing his review as "the harshest" *U.S. 1* received. He goes on to relate Wheelwright's review to the "Rukeyser imbroglio" of the 1940s, the occasion for which was Rukeyser's work in the Office of War Information during World War II and her essay about war posters, "Words and Images," published in the *New Republic*, August 2, 1943. In a brief article in the September-October 1943 issue of *Partisan Review*, Rukeyser was accused of a variety of offenses, including opportunism and a lack of political conviction. The article, "Grandeur and Misery of a Poster Girl," was signed "R.S.P.," presumably the initials of *Partisan Review* editors Philip Rahv, Delmore Schwartz, and William Phillips. According to Dwight Macdonald, Schwartz was the principal author. Rukeyser was defended in the pages of the magazine by Rebecca Pitts ("The Rukeyser Imbroglio" [winter 1944]), and F. O. Matthiessen ("The Rukeyser Imbroglio Cont'd" [spring 1944]). This, however, was a controversy that had no discernible relation to the content of Wheelwright's review, and to which Wheelwright, who died in 1940, was obviously not a party ("Documentary Modernism").

of the economic. Thus Kalaidjian rebukes Wheelwright for "his desire to penetrate to capital's essence, and thus bypass the discursive war of representations mediating class struggle," a discursive war in which *The Book of the Dead*, Kalaidjian argues, is firmly enlisted. But, as I noted above, "excrescences" refers not to ideological emanations, but rather to extreme and sensational cases of capitalist abuse, as opposed to capitalism's routine functioning and systemic properties. Kalaidjian's desire to promote Rukeyser within terms acceptable to contemporary critical discourse leads him to overemphasize Rukeyser's feminism—a real, though not in my opinion decisive, component of *The Book of the Dead*—and to misread Wheelwright's review, reading it in the terms of contemporary literary theory rather than those of classical Marxism. (Kalaidjian's attribution of Wheelwright's hostility to *The Book of the Dead* to antifeminism is particularly problematical because of Wheelwright's praise for the *Night-Music* section of *U.S. 1*, in which feminism is arguably more prominent than in *The Book of the Dead*.)

In his eagerness to read *The Book of the Dead* as the product of a Foucaultian "specific intellectual," Kalaidjian makes a number of relatively minor errors with regard to the specifics of Rukeyser's poem. Thus, his interesting and provocative comments are marred by a number of oversights. He refers to "Union Carbide's ruthless mining practices," when what was being constructed was primarily a tunnel; mistakenly reports the length of the tunnel as three-quarters of a mile rather than 3¾ miles; refers to Willard Maas, a member of the Communist party, as a member of the political Right; misrepresents Maas's comment about poetry "modeled after leaflets"; refers to Karl Kautsky and George Plekhanov, both Marxist intellectuals of the Second International, as Communists; appears to conflate the Second International with the Third Period of the Third International; refers to "universal expressions of resistance on both the left and the right" to *The Book of the Dead*; mistakes White Sulphur Springs in "The Road" for Gauley Bridge; and refers to Vivian Jones as a "contaminated worker," when there is no evidence that he personally suffered from silicosis. As with his reaction to Wheelwright, so too in his more general treatment of *The Book of the Dead* Kalaidjian sacrifices the integrity of the object of investigation to the demands of his thesis.

To disagree with Kertesz and Kalaidjian is not necessarily to agree with Wheelwright, although Wheelwright's stated opinions deserve more respect than Kertesz and Kalaidjian are inclined to show them. That Rukeyser herself respected Wheelwright's opinions may be seen in her failure to react to Wheelwright's review in the way one would expect if Kertesz's or Kalaidjian's characterizations of it were correct. According to Alan Wald, "Muriel, in fact, was not especially upset by the review and saw

Wheelwright as her teacher, and was still reading him when I last saw her, very shortly before her death."[16] While Rukeyser spoke with Wald in the late 1970s, her comments at that time do not appear to be a retrospective revision on her part. She sent a draft of her poem *The Soul and Body of John Brown* to Wheelwright for his comments after his *Partisan Review* piece was published. Wheelwright retyped the draft (badly), incorporating his revisions, and appended a handwritten note: "Perhaps if you study this repulsive draft it will open up possibilities of revisions. I do not think your poem is worked out yet[.] You are full of talent and seriousness; but you are loose. Scrutinise and search." Rukeyser wrote to Wheelwright about his revisions: "Thank you for the illumination. Some of it was absolutely right and I have made many changes with it as starting-point. . . . It was the ability to shake it free (of some of the style that still swamps me and that I am trying to get rid of) that your letter gave me." Similarly, to Louis Untermeyer she wrote: "I've rewritten the *Brown*. Jack Wheelwright sent me *his* version of it and it shook me loose. I hadn't been able to do it before."[17] While Rukeyser thought more highly of her "Gauley Bridge poems" than did Wheelwright, she did not feel that their difference of opinion marked any kind of serious rupture between them.

What, then, accounts for Wheelwright's review? Wheelwright's dislike of *The Book of the Dead*—he was very favorably inclined toward *Night-Music* ("Here is a poem no capitalist would write")—stemmed from at least two sources. First, he objected to the technique of *The Book of the Dead*. He found the poem to lack clarity, to rely too much on "the oblique manners" of modern poetry. In an elaboration appended to the manuscript of his review, but that was unfortunately not printed in the *Partisan Review* (see Appendix II), he asserted:

> These manners depend entirely upon sensorial effect, they show a distrust of intellectual effect, which is a chief part of all literature and the chiefest part of revolutionary literature, for a mere stirring of sense and feeling without intellectual direction, would leave our public defenceless before the stirring demagogy of counter-revolution.[18]

Wheelwright condemns the oblique manner for overemphasizing sensorial impressions without providing an intellectual context within which to understand them. This is a problem especially for revolutionary literature

16. Alan Wald, letter to author, March 27, 1998.

17. Wheelwright to Rukeyser, n.d., Rukeyser Papers; Rukeyser to Wheelwright, June 4, 1940, Wheelwright Collection; Rukeyser to Untermeyer, June 9, 1940, Louis Untermeyer Collection, University of Delaware.

18. John Wheelwright, "Muriel Rukeyser—U.S. 1," typescript, Wheelwright Collection.

because the intellectual context it requires is not that of the "common sense" of a capitalist society. Unlike non- or counterrevolutionary art, it cannot rely on the reader to summon up the appropriate intellectual context by default. Hence, "sensorial impressionism" is not an appropriate method for the leftist poet.

Wheelwright contrasts the oblique manner with the straightforwardly narrative—but hardly artless—method of Longfellow in "The Midnight Ride of Paul Revere," which he calls "a paradigm of a conjugation of political narrative poetry. Actually bare of any content but the most poetically abstract, it tells all readers everything, but yet closes with what winning courtesy, telling us we already knew it all!"[19] Wheelwright's emphasis on the necessity of including intellectual content in revolutionary poetry and his understanding of Longfellow's poem are astute, and suggest Antonio Gramsci's analysis of hegemony as well as Gramsci's deep interest, expressed in numerous articles for *Avanti!* and *Le Ordine Nuovo*, in the social and political dimensions of popular culture. The hegemonic culture, according to Gramsci, determines what counts as "common sense," the passive repository of accepted norms and "knowledge" that "everyone knows."[20] A revolutionary art cannot rely upon this passive repository and therefore, one could argue on a Gramscian basis, must supply an intellectual framework not required by other types of art. Taken on their own terms, and with an appreciation of their resonance, Wheelwright's opinions and analyses are not without interest.

And yet one need not conclude that the nonnarrative method of *The Book of the Dead* presents a decisive political-aesthetic problem. That it is not a narrative poem Rukeyser noted in her radio interview:

> I think that it would be misleading to describe my poem as narrative poetry in the ordinary sense. I have tried to write a series of poems which are linked together as the sequences of a movie are linked together . . . so that during the sequence the reader has built up for him the story and the picture. . . .
> I should say that there are two ways of telling a story . . . the one that is used in the novel and the theater, which is the method of straight development and unfolding of the story . . . and the other that of the movies and some contemporary long poems: for example, Hart Crane's *The Bridge* and Horace Gregory's *Chorus for Survival*. In this second technique, relationships are made clear in the same way that a movie shot of a city being bombed will show you first a picture of the plane dropping its bomb . . . and then will cut away to the ground and the explosion itself. The movie public has adjusted itself to this sequence so that there isn't any strain or lack of belief in the tie-up between the two pictures. And in the same way, readers of contemporary

19. Wheelwright, "U.S. 1," page 5a of typescript.
20. Antonio Gramsci, *Selections from the Cultural Writings*, 20–86, and *Selections from the Prison Notebooks*, 198–99, 323–33.

poetry are finding that the adjustment of this kind of writing makes for vivid and active poetry.[21]

Rukeyser clearly alludes to montage as an alternative to narrative as a method for uniting the various elements in a long work. Indeed, in her major statement on poetics, *The Life of Poetry* (1949), she refers directly to Sergei Eisenstein, chief theorist of montage, and it is quite possible that she read his essay "Through Theatre to Cinema" in *Theatre Arts Monthly*. The essay was published in the September 1936 issue, and would thus have been current while she was working on *The Book of the Dead*.[22]

Rukeyser does not appear to evaluate narrative and montage as forms that are inherently political *as forms*. Rather, she discusses them as methods of presentation and evaluates them accordingly: montage appeals to her as a means toward producing "vivid and active poetry." It is appealing for aesthetic reasons that, while not necessarily irrelevant to the political dimension of a work, she does not immediately identify with that dimension. Wheelwright's preference for narrative presentation, on the other hand, appears to stem from an implicit identification of the obliqueness of montage with an unwanted political consequence. Because montage functions through unstated connections between sensorial impressions that appear to be discrete, it lacks the ability of narrative to stage an argument, as well as the direction that produces an "intellectual effect, which is a chief part of all literature and the chiefest part of revolutionary literature." Montage, as characterized by Wheelwright, is thus ill-suited to the needs of the leftist writer.

However, it can be argued that montage is politically preferable to narrative construction; as Rukeyser was no doubt aware, Eisenstein himself made this argument. Whereas narrative traditionally delivers a work to the audience in a closed, finished form, montage presents a series of images that the audience must combine itself. Montage thus produces an active audience, while narrative produces a passive audience. An active audience is politically preferable; therefore, montage is politically preferable to narrative. Such an argument, in various forms, is by now quite familiar. Yet, despite the fact that many a polemical struggle has been fought over the matter, one need not choose sides with either narrative or montage. Brecht, no stranger to this debate, offers a salutary antidote to the tendency to see

21. Rukeyser, interview with Sillen.
22. Essays by, interviews with, and articles about Eisenstein were widely available to the English-reading public beginning in the late 1920s in places where Rukeyser was likely to see them: the *Nation, Daily Worker, New Republic, New York Times, Life and Letters Today,* and others. Rukeyser's interest in Eisenstein is attested to also by her translation of Arthur Rimbaud's "Voyelles," prepared for *The Film Sense,* a collection of translations of Eisenstein essays.

any given aesthetic form as the bearer of truth: "When it comes to literary forms, one must question reality, not aesthetics, not even the aesthetics of realism. There are many ways in which truth can be concealed and many ways in which it can be told."[23]

Whatever the merits of Wheelwright's objections to the method that unites *The Book of the Dead*, his difference of opinion with Rukeyser concerning montage is not the only, and possibly not the most important, difference between them, and this brings us to the second basis on which Wheelwright rejects *The Book of the Dead*. Wheelwright misread the poem largely because of his fundamental failure to grasp the temporal plane on which the poem functions, to sense the *mode* of "scientific socialism" within which Rukeyser was working. When Wheelwright objects that Rukeyser ignores capitalism's "inner nature," "makes no root attack upon everyday exploitation," and fails to show how capitalism's "doom is sealed in the pay envelope," he assumes that Rukeyser means to attack capitalism as a mode of production whose fundamental mechanism ("inner nature") is the extraction of surplus value through the ordinary economic functions of social interaction.[24] This theory of capitalist society—elaborated in *Das Kapital*—is without a doubt one of the signal accomplishments of Marx. Yet it is not the only mode in which Marxist theory, or Marx himself, operates.

The difference between Wheelwright and Rukeyser at this point stems from Wheelwright's reading *The Book of the Dead* through the conceptual schema of Marx's "special theory" of capitalist society; Rukeyser, however, wrote *The Book of the Dead* within the conceptual register of Marx's "general theory" of human society. This distinction between special theory and general theory within Marxism, while it dates back to Engels, has been developed and refined by Keith Graham. Graham holds that the special theory is Marx's attempt to explain in detail the fundamental principles and dynamics specific to the epoch in which he lived, to capitalism. Marx's general theory of human society attempts to provide a theory of the nature of human societies in general, according to which the economic is invariably determinate in the last instance, while the specific principles and dynamics of any given society may vary widely.[25] On the basis of this conception of societies, the general theory also includes a theory of history, and it is on this historical rather than structural axis—as is clear from the conclusions of "The Dam" and "The Book of the Dead," especially—that *The Book of the Dead* operates.

One can see the broad outlines of *The Book of the Dead* in Graham's summary of the vision of history produced by Marx's general theory:

23. Brecht quoted in Galvano Della Volpe, *Critique of Taste*, 239.
24. Wheelwright, "U.S. 1," 55.
25. Keith Graham, *Karl Marx, Our Contemporary: Social Theory for a Post-Leninist World*, 5–8, 41–117.

Accumulation of productive forces is not a smooth progression; it emerges not from the deliberations of rational individuals somehow detached from their class locations, but from a clash between interest groups where vital interests are at stake: a release of life for the exploiting class, who will not have to forfeit a proportion of their life working to produce for their own needs; a loss of life for the exploited class, who will have to forfeit a greater proportion of their own life to provide for others' needs as well as their own. With so much at stake, it is little wonder that epochal transformation produces social convulsion.[26]

And yet, history, within the general theory and within *The Book of the Dead*, is not just a dismal tale of luxury and leisure for some and domination and misery for others, precisely because there is a tendency for the "accumulation of productive forces," and the possibility of their coming under the control of the exploited and dominated: "Their hands touched mastery."

History, referred to somewhat cryptically at the beginning of this discussion, thus emerges as the crucial term omitted from Wheelwright's consideration of Rukeyser's poem. Wheelwright simply got wrong the vein of scientific socialism within which Rukeyser works in *The Book of the Dead*, a failure attributable neither to a fundamental difference in perspectives between Wheelwright and Rukeyser nor to Wheelwright's supposedly sexist, Marxist, modernist hostility to Rukeyser's supposedly (proto-)Foucaultian, feminist, postmodernist poetics. *Both* Wheelwright and Rukeyser are Marxist *and* modernist poets.

26. Ibid., 78.

6

The Book of the Dead:
A Vision of History

In his interesting and intelligent discussion of *The Book of the Dead*, Michael Davidson comments on the use of the term *mastery* in "Absalom" (82):

> *I have gained mastery over my heart*
> *I have gained mastery over my two hands*
> *I have gained mastery over the waters*
> *I have gained mastery over the river.*

> In a poem in which individuals have ceded power to the power company, such claims of mastery appear to have been made in vain. But when the mother's voice is joined to the testimony of others—Rukeyser's as well—then some of the suffering may be mitigated.[1]

Davidson's point is sound as far as it goes. Yet it is symptomatic—not only of Davidson's reading of the poem, but of the general literary-critical sensibility—that the relief of suffering, the sense of reconciliation or vindication that the critic discerns, is of a purely verbal or discursive character and, furthermore, insofar as one may imagine the issue of "voice" to have real-world consequences, is sharply qualified, even muted: "*some* of the suffering *may* be *mitigated*." At one level this is unobjectionable—after all, it is a *poem* we are dealing with. Yet my argument throughout this analysis of *The Book of the Dead* is that Rukeyser was playing for higher stakes than this. The terrain on which her poem ultimately fights is that of history, and her vision of history is at its deepest levels informed by Marxism.

1. Michael Davidson, *Ghostlier Demarcations: Modern Poetry and the Material Word*, 145.

But openly confronting the Marxist underpinnings of *The Book of the Dead* would prove difficult for the overwhelming majority of contemporary literary critics, for whom Marxism appears to be at best one theoretical and interpretive option among others, and at worst a superannuated, superseded, and totalitarian discourse. This creates a dilemma: a fundamental component of *The Book of the Dead*, a Marxist theory of history, seems particularly unattractive to most critics, except in the most limited and provisional ways. Thus the sensibility of someone like Rukeyser, otherwise so appealing and so worthy of recovery, remains alien in a fundamental aspect and is both misunderstood and misrepresented. One could, of course, dodge the political bullet by making the historicist argument that a Marxist vision of history underpins *The Book of the Dead* just as Aquinas's vision of the cosmos underpins *The Divine Comedy.* Yet such a maneuver, while not factually incorrect, blunts the force of Rukeyser's poem, radically altering the demands it makes upon us. Instead of making this essentially antiquarian historicist argument, I will not only assert that Marxism is the view that underpins *The Book of the Dead* but I would also argue for the continuing vitality of the theory of history that informs and animates Rukeyser's poem.

In an eloquent and concise restatement of Marx's view of history that speaks directly to the aspect of Marx's theory that figures most prominently in *The Book of the Dead*, Jeffrey Vogel notes that in all of the defenses of capitalism and attacks on Marxism that have been penned, precious little evidence has been offered that capitalism does not possess all the destructive tendencies that Marxists have customarily identified: stunting lives that are subordinated to the imperatives of the market, encouraging racial and national conflicts, destroying the environment, and offering the prospect of nuclear holocaust. "If these basic facts are still true," Vogel offers, "then we should expect the people relatively most harmed by capitalism to take action against it, to the extent that they are able, since people tend to judge harms in relative and relational terms. The people who have the largest overlap of ability and interest . . . in opposing capitalism remains the working class as Marxism has traditionally defined it."[2] The intellectual framework undergirding *The Book of the Dead*, Vogel's argument implies, retains its purchase on reality.

Vogel further argues that, as a consequence of its purchase on reality, Marxism—specifically Marx's vision of history—retains its purchase on us:

> It may be that those who reject Marx's views on the revolutionary potential of the working class are correct. But then it is incumbent upon them to offer a more coherent account of social change. Otherwise, they will have no reason to rejoice that the human species will do any better than it has so

2. Vogel, "Tragedy of History," 61.

far. . . . Marx's account of [the] revolutionary potential of the working class, whatever its difficulties, remains the most generally coherent solution yet proposed to the problems that remain with us. For these reasons, we may rationally believe, with Marx, that the working class will end the tragedy of human progress and thereby bring "the pre-history of human society to a close."[3]

If Vogel's bracing restatement of Marx's vision of history is correct, *The Book of the Dead* is not merely of historical interest, but also makes a claim on us as readers in the present.

However, the nature of a poem such as *The Book of the Dead* differs considerably from that of the statement of a theory of history, and the relationship between these two different types of discourse is not immediately clear. A useful way to approach this problem is through the distinction between a *theory* and a *philosophy* of history, particularly as it relates to Marxist historiography, a distinction that has been explored at length by Alex Callinicos and Eero Loone. For present purposes, it will suffice to note that philosophers of history start, so to speak, by ascribing a meaning to history which they then illustrate by reference to particular events which, they believe, demonstrate that the meaning they impute to history is in fact unfolding within it. Theories of history share some characteristics of philosophies of history: they both cover an extensive range of time, rather than the more limited segments of history characteristic of what has become standard historical research, and "they seek to offer universal mechanisms responsible for historical change." However, theories "do not seek to discover the meaning of the historical process, if by that is meant providing some judgment of its overall moral significance."[4] Unlike philosophies of history, theories of history are scientific in nature and distinguish between, rather than conflate, moral judgment and causal explanation.

The Book of the Dead is clearly not the statement or restatement of a theory of history; it shares an emphasis on meaning characteristic of philosophies of history and is thus seemingly incompatible with Marxism as a scientific theory of history. But this is merely to say that *The Book of the Dead* is not itself an example of Marxism as a scientific theory of history, that it is not a research program. As a poem, *The Book of the Dead* simply does something different from works such as Perry Anderson's *Lineages of the Absolutist*

3. Ibid.
4. Alex Callinicos, *Theories and Narratives: Reflections on the Philosophy of History*, 41. See also Eero Loone, *Soviet Marxism and Analytical Philosophies of History*. In addition, Bhaskar's *Possibility of Naturalism* and Andrew Collier's *Scientific Realism and Socialist Thought* have influenced my thinking on the nature of scientific explanation in history and its relation to decidedly nonscientific texts, such as *The Book of the Dead*, that engage with history.

State or Guy Bois's *The Crisis of Feudalism*. The distinction between philosophy of history and theory of history does not imply that inquiry into meaning in history is invalid or illegitimate. It simply indicates that one should permit causal explanation to precede moral judgment.[5] Looked at in this fashion, Rukeyser's poem can be seen to present a vision of history built upon a theory of history.

As a vision of history, *The Book of the Dead* inquires into the meaning of history as it presents itself to Rukeyser. It is at this point, where we move from the naked fact of the tunnel workers' deaths to the meaning of those deaths, that the otherwise quite ambiguous mythological dimension of the poem must be located. If it is the potential for emancipation, for "mastery" of the conditions of existence, that the vision of history in *The Book of the Dead* offers, then it is myth that helps to deliver the events of the Gauley Tunnel tragedy to the bar of history. By constructing a mythic level within the poem Rukeyser is more readily able to animate a sense of redemption, which is simultaneously mythic and historical. The specific character of this redemptive vision is well explained by Callinicos: "The suffering consequent on the development of the productive forces is not denied or explained away; at best it may be redeemed when revolution allows the victims of progress, or their proletarian descendants, to take control of these forces."[6] The mythological character of the poem may be reconciled with the historical vision upon which it is based so long as we recognize that as a poem, *The Book of the Dead* answers to different demands than does a scientific theory of history. While a scientific theory of history attempts to offer the most complete explanation of events and dynamics in the form of empirical evidence, a vision of history transforms a theory of history by adding to it both a moral and an aesthetic register, whereby the sense of history generated within the theory may be *felt* as well as known.

This distinction between theories and visions of history helps us also to understand the relationship between myth and history in *The Book of the Dead*, since it clarifies the enhanced role of the moral and the aesthetic in visions of history. By their very nature as composites, visions of history are less tidy intellectual constructs than are theories. The level at which myth and history join in *The Book of the Dead* is thus of necessity rather muddy. Yet some clarity may be gained if we try to understand the nature of cultural objects, such as *The Book of the Dead*, that (quite consciously, in the present case) attempt to place human experience within a meaningful intellectual-emotional framework.

An illuminating attempt to provide a schema for understanding the complex ways in which people interpret their own and other's existence may be

---

5. Callinicos, *Theories and Narratives*, 42.
6. Ibid., 163.

found in Goran Therborn's delineation of the "universe of ideological inter-pellations." Therborn differentiates four ideological modes, two of which concern us here. The "inclusive-existential" mode of ideology attempts to explain the place of humanity as a whole, as a species, in the universe; this would seem to describe myth, as well as religion. "Positional-historical" ideologies attempt to explain one's membership in groups in relation to others, or within a social structure. This accords with common uses of the term *ideology*, and would describe, for example, the relationship between workers and capitalists. Rukeyser's mythologizing in *The Book of the Dead* seems to participate in both of these ideological modes, which is hardly unusual since, as Therborn notes, his distinctions are of an analytical char-acter: any concrete ideology typically mobilizes more than one mode at a time. Thus, he writes: "The meaning of a person's life and world is an exis-tential question not wholly answerable by reference to the relations of pro-duction, but rather addressed by the inclusive-existential ideologies of reli-gious and secular morality."[7] Rukeyser's limited use of mythical elements may therefore be seen to emerge from and to acknowledge the multidi-mensionality of human subjectivity and the inexorable demand to consider moral questions in order to address the inescapable problem of meaning. It is, after all, a profound moral problem to try to comprehend the meaning of such events as the Gauley Tunnel tragedy, as it is to try to comprehend the meaning of a history in which such events are hardly uncommon. Ulti-mately, then, the significance of *The Book of the Dead* lies in the way in which it addresses these problems.

7. Goran Therborn, *The Ideology of Power and the Power of Ideology*, 23, 26.

Appendix

I. "Silicosis in Our Town," by Martha Millet

Martha Millet's "Silicosis in Our Town" appeared in the *Daily Worker*, June 2, 1936. Millet, who was about eighteen at the time, went on to write *Thine Alabaster Cities: A Poem for Our Times* (Brooklyn: n.p., 1952) and *Dangerous Jack: A Fantasy in Verse* (New York: Sierra Press, 1953). She also edited *The Rosenbergs: Poems of the United States* (New York: Sierra Press, 1957) and contributed to *Seven Poets in Search of an Answer: Maxwell Bodenheim, Joy Davidman, Langston Hughes, Aaron Kramer, Alfred Kreymborg, Martha Millet, Norman Rosten*, ed. Thomas Yoseloff (New York, B. Ackerman, 1944). Millet was married to leftist journalist Sender Garlin until his death in 1999. Permission to reprint "Silicosis in Our Town" was granted by Martha Millet Garlin.

> Silicosis in Our Town
>
> One day that old man Bones he come
> A-knockin' at my door—
> Now Charlie Jones give heed 'cause you
> Ain't gonna live much more.
>
> For I was cold and weary
> And I was hungry too
> So I went into that mountain
> To drill the tunnel through.
>
> The water that they gave us
> It was covered up with white
> And the dust so thick in front of you
> You couldn't see no light.
>
> My youngest son he died there
> And he was but eighteen.

O folks it is the saddest thing
A father's ever seen.

But ere he closed his eyes he said—
Please cut me open wide;
O father dear and mother dear,
Find out what's wrong inside—.

His lungs was hard and withered
There was no room for air,
He died from a dread sickness
That he got while working there.

Twice more we sat and prayed there
And could not go to sleep.
It breaks a father's heart to see
His sons die out like sheep.

The Union Carbide Company
They sent us into that gloom.
Two thousand good and strong men
They sent right to their doom.

It was twenty million dollars
That tunnel cost to crash,
But the lives of common workingmen
Are cheap as any trash.

They did not spend a penny
To save our life and health.
They did not lift a finger
While we made their bloody wealth.

Well, folks we gave our labor
And did our best to please
And now us men are dead and dying
Of that dread disease.

It gets into your body and
It eats your lungs away.
This dreaded silicosis
It makes you choke all day.

Five hundred men have passed away
A-gaspin' for their breath
And fifteen hundred more are sentenced
To a living death.

They dumped them in a cornfield
They crowded them right close

They did not even wash their hands
Or change their working clothes.

Now often you may see their loved ones
Seeking them at dark.
Their bones lie in that cornfield
And those graves they have no mark.

I wake up in the morning,
And I go to bed at night,
And folks, that old man Bones he lies
Right down there by my side.

How can I eat, how can I sleep
How can I face the sun?
A man feels lowdown when his days
Are numbered every one.

A man with silicosis cannot work
How hard he tries—
O must he see his wife and children
Starve before his eyes?

Say brother in that cornfield
Move over just a pace.
It won't be long but I'll be comin' round
To claim my place.

You folks who think that human lives
Are worth far more than gold,
To the Union Carbide Company
You must raise your voices bold.

You women folks and mothers
Who love your dearest ones,
You must speak out for the lives
Of your husbands and your sons.

II. "Muriel Rukeyser—U.S. 1," by John Wheelwright

John Wheelwright's review "Muriel Rukeyser—U.S. 1" appears in typescript in the John Wheelwright Collection, John Hay Library, Brown University, by whose permission it is reproduced here. The version of the review published in *Partisan Review* 4:4 (March 1938) differs from the typescript in several places. It is unclear whether the revisions reached the editors late, were never sent, or were ignored. Material not found in the published review appears below in boldface (with the exception of misspellings that the *Partisan Review* editors simply corrected).

"Muriel Rukeyser—U.S. 1"

Among the poets born under the World War, Rukeyser, able and ambitious, has assimilated the prosodic taste and social philosophy which were worked out then. They are being worn **thin** now and, for all her straightforward perception, they disable her when she is most ambitious. Her full ability appears in lesser pieces, not in the title poems of *Theory of Flight* and *U.S. 1* which fall below the high standards they raise up against themselves. The shorter pieces show that in longer poems she may yet do what she wants and, apprehending contemporary fact through immediate documentation, compel instant sense of moral history. The mere attempt is generous to our poetic growth.

Poetry develops intuitive reason not by logical contrivances so much as by immediate sensual association. This is so delightful a process to follow that a poet easily wins readers over to his teaching, if only he be clear about what he has to say and whom he has to address. Given proper audiences, poets are the best agitators: but no one ever has an audience given to him; we must win our own by what we sound and show and teach. All poetry's sound and show is subservient to its teaching even if what it teaches is just what it sounds and shows (i.e. "Pure" Poetry). Where poems are stuttered and blurred, it is because their authors do not know what they are about.

Rukeyser refers to social revolution but tells little of its purpose or method; yet this is just what people want to learn. Though she says, "Say 'Yes,' people, say 'Yes Yes,'" one can hear "the" people answering "Oh yeah?".

Her socialism belongs to the inexperienced school—pre-war. Philispphic [sic] experience, necessary to any agitation except that Debs called "agitation of the atmosphere," is necessary above all to a choice of super-image. For *Theory of Flight* she chose the flying machine because it consumates historic effort and, extending the body through space-time, opens up a vaster spread for reason and imagination; and Freed men will do all this for a world society; yet the super-image is intractable. Process of flight is not an accurate equivalent to process of emancipation. The overtones of flight imply escapism (Get out from under home and father). The sensations of flight dreamily translate into fornicating. "Yes," she says, "Yes," she says, "Do." No, rebellious individuals who made the revolution sexy, long have freed capitalist culture from bourgeois decorum. Edna Millay is a sexual saint of the Women's Clubs. All of this may well be good. But it is not the revolved love we expect to enjoy after the abolition of property, and, at its best, is only tangent to proletarian concern. Free sexes will be by-products of a more impersonal engineering. The delayed adolescence of this century holds down *Theory of Flight*.

The highroad, *U.S. 1*, is a more tractable super-image, for its overtones imply not escape *from*, but passage *to*. Possibly it is laid down to carry too much traffic which might as well stay at home. We cannot tell; only a detour has been completed; the freight has scarcely got under way. But no more than *Theory of Flight* does *U.S. 1* give people what is good to hear. Its *Book of the Dead* tells how the Union Carbide Company in cutting costs killed off carload after carload of workers by filling them [*sic*] lungs full with glass powder which they had them drill dry out of a hydraulic superconduit, and sold at a good price. This abomination needs to be made memorable. But as not one line of its thousand lines describes the wage system a goodly number of poetry readers will say, "We haven't the remotest why anyone but a dumb cluck worked there. It's a free country, isn't it?" The poem attacks the excrescencies [*sic*] of capitalism, not the system's inner nature. Like any good capitalist, Rukeyser condemns bad, shockingly bad, working conditions, but makes no root attack upon everyday exploitation. Capital, the parasite is parricide. Yet not a line of all this condemnation shows its doom is sealed in the pay envelope. **The poet has missed the point. Inherited pre-War revision of scientific socialism, which Stalin's pre-War [*sic*] revision meets more than halfway, makes it impossible for her to go on and do her work.**

Work left undone, *Theory of Flight* accomplished a rebellion (against parental super-annuation and the unseemly avoirdupois of kept women and sugar daddies) by that resentment, irrelevant but so distracting, under whose spell poems, like cartoons, decline from symbolism to idolatry, Devil-Boss and Worker-Saint. The Negro problem presents firmer poetic material than prostitution does. The close of Rukeyser's *George Robinson Blues* verges on symbolism where a negro says:

> **As dark as I am, when I came out to [*sic*] morning after the tunnel at night**
> **with a white man, nobody could have told which man was white.**
> **The dust had covered us both, and the dust was white.**

This dust in truth is the wage-profit system; but in the poem it is merely silica poisoning, and the verse is allegory.

A limited philosophy limits poetry; political and aesthetic failings have one root. Her genius, knowing that "poetry can extend the document," guided [her] to the Egyptian *Book of the Dead* and to the *Congressional Record;* but the rewriting does not click. The verse slips from the fulcrum balance through sound and time of parallel or contrasting thoughts which, even in a machine line, constitutes verse. There are many portraits of the worker victims; none strike to the heart, for unscientific socialism, which shares only in the bourgeois' humanity, is more moved by lads without jobs than by men with jobs. How well she can draw when stirred is shown in a separate portrait of an unemployed boy who has his sister give him a short haircut so that he can go out and get some work to do. But she shows no such understanding of the wage system as Emerson shows in his *Chartist's*

Complaint, that magical confounding of all nature with class struggle. Consequently, the vision of white dust through which workers drill swiftly to their deaths, for all the abstract terror of its sharp line and value, is out of scale like the landscape of *The Slave in the Dismal Swamp* of Longfellow who, knowing less about exploitation than she, was likewise distracted from the difficult human to easy nature.

Yet Longfellow knew much. Not merely small points, how to rhyme where we inclined toward mutiners [muteness], but big points of methodology. He is remarkable. *Paul Revere's Ride* is a paradigm of a conjugation of political narrative poetry. Actually bare of any content but the most poetically abstract, it tells all readers everything, but yet closes with what winning courtesy, telling us we already knew it all! In every particular, what a contrast it makes to the prevailing manners, whose purposes are, precisely, *not* to tell a story. **These manners depend entirely upon sensorial effect, they show a distrust of intellectual effect, which is a chief part of all literature and the chiefest part of revolutionary literature, for a mere stirring of sense and feeling without intellectual direction, would leave our public defenceless before the stirring demagogy of counter-revolution.**

Furthermore the method of sensorial impressionism has run itself to seed. Laura Riding, a mistress of the oblique manner, leaves the story of her *Laura and Francisca* quite untold. The result is diverting, but not really interesting except to people who have read too many detective stories. In *John and I* she sets out, much like Pirandello in his *Six Characters in Search of an Author*, to recount a story which has no inner consistency. This is interesting at first until she says "Then strip the narrative of mystery." From then on, the whole thing falls to pieces. At the close we agree with her that *John and I* are better off like this,—with the story left untold.

> **"But lest we tell only half, fear to know all**
> **Lest all should be to tell."**

As Disraeli on his deathbed stated "If I had been a Nihilist, I would have told all" so Laura Riding, a most significant though minor representative of a contemporary manner of narrative poetry, like an inhibited patient who cannot tell the truth has reached the empasse [sic] of fearing "lest all should be to tell." The time has come for a right-about-face:

> **"Exchange the multiplied bewilderment**
> **for a singlr [sic] presentation of fact by fairness**
> **and the revelation will be instantaneous."**

A literature lies before us in the rediscovery of clarity. Practitioners of the oblique manners, unlike Longfellow, do not flatter our self esteem, making us feel bright, meeting us with knowledge, but rather do they browbeat us by making us feel stupid even before their rude erudition. They deal with such open or closed secrets as compel a dislocation of the hierarchy of governing and subordinating clauses which would be the envy of a Statler Hotel after-dinner speaker, did they not contrive a more offensive tone of snob superiority. This taste is so alien to Rukeyser's purpose that she is a least offender but her least, nonetheless, harms her work. Particularly when it goes telegraphic and lets the subject, object, verb be taken for granted, or at any rate, omitted. Such methods rise under the accepted canon of culture of the ruling class, but, where the purpose be to win adherents from across classes to an unaccepted cannon, they do only for subjects (love, death etc.) where stores of reference are available to anyone. Rukeyser's exquisite *Night Music,* from private reference, reaches bold revolutionary conclusion. Here is a poem no capitalist would write. *The Cruise* in 18 pages of nice evocations of the *Flying Dutchman* and the *Hunting of the Snark* leaves undone what is done in one page of the third movement of *Night Music.*

Phillistines unsnubbed would dismiss the poem as obscure. That is because it recognizes mysteries and wrestles with them, which is a different matter from willful mystification, although indistinguishable to persons who have stultified their interior references. Poets need care little if they be called obscure by Phillistines. One political use of poetry is to single out the body of the elect, but if poetry actually is obscure it fails; and in our age, when economic contradictions are charged with many meanings and society is confronted with a choice of futures, obscurity is a natural characteristic of literature which wise writers must work against, and most especially in social revolutionary subject matter. All things long pursued lead through that door. Leave the timid their obscurity. Confront communication. It devolves upon us to rediscover clarity. Revolutionary writing in the snob style does not reach a proper audience. We can find **ensamples** in no academic bourgeois decay, but in experimental masters of all rising classes that struggled through the centuries for mastery.

III. Radio interview of Muriel Rukeyser by Samuel Sillen

This typescript of a radio interview between Muriel Rukeyser and Samuel Sillen is housed in the Berg Collection, New York Public Library, by whose permission it is reproduced here. It is undated, though it was obviously conducted in early 1938, and there is no indication on which station it was broadcast. A handwritten note at the top of the typescript reads: "For Muriel—who wrote it. Sam," so we may assume that the questions were Rukeyser's and not Sillen's. The typescript also includes a few handwritten corrections and additions, which are silently incorporated into the version below.

Sillen: It is a pleasure to introduce to the radio audience this afternoon one of America's most gifted young poets. Miss Muriel Rukeyser has just published her second volume of verse: *U.S. 1*. Her first volume—*Theory of Flight*—was published two years ago. That volume, one of the most impressive to be issued in the Yale University Younger Poet[s] series, was universally hailed by the critics as an outstanding achievement. William Rose Benét, writing in the *Saturday Review of Literature*, said:

> This young woman is only twenty-one years old and her work is full of vigor and fire . . . When you hold this book in your hand you hold a living thing . . . You are at once struck by the fact that here is something new, something real and alive, of our time and our own day. If the bitterness of our day is here, the hope of it is here also: the new youth that is already rising and shining.

Lewis Gannett of the *Herald-Tribune* pointed out that the *Theory of Flight* has ["]as fresh a tone as any American poetry of the year." And Horace Gregory wrote in the *New Republic:* "If there is hope for poetry in contemporary England, the poetry of Muriel Rukeyser has also made it plain that the same hope is visible in America."[1]

Such high praise from leading critics is not often bestowed on a first book of verse. And this is all the more striking in the case of such a young writer as Miss Rukeyser, who, incidentally, is the youngest poet included in Louis Unterm[e]yer's anthology of Modern American Poetry.

Miss Rukeyser was born in New York City, December 15, 1913. She attended Vassar and Columbia. Since she does not believe that poetry can be spun out of a vacuum, she has attempted to experience her subject matter before writing about it. Thus she worked her way through the ground course at Roosevelt Aviation School before writing her *Theory of Flight*. She visited Alabama before writing her famous poem on Scottsboro. Her poem on Gauley Bridge, which forms an important section of her new book[,] is also based on personal observation. In 1936 she went to England, from where a London magazine sent her to report the People's Olympics in Barcelona, which were to open, as you may recall, on the day the Spanish Civil War began. Two long poems in the present book are based on that experience.

But I see that Miss Rukeyser is getting rather impatient with my chatter about her personal history. It is always one of the embarrassments of the

---

1. William Rose Benét, review of *U.S. 1*, *Saturday Review of Literature*, December 7, 1935, 47; Lewis Gannett, review of *U.S. 1*, *New York Herald-Tribune*, date unknown; Horace Gregory, "A Hope for Poetry," review of *U.S. 1*, *New Republic*, February 5, 1936, 374.

critic that he has to dig into other people's lives without even getting their permission . . . So let us turn to the book itself . . . Miss Rukeyser, do you mind explaining the significance of the title which you have selected for your new book?

Rukeyser: Not at all, Dr. Sillen. The title stands, quite simply, for the federal highway—U.S. 1—which runs along the Atlantic Coast, from Maine to Florida. I plan to write a summary poem of the life of the Atlantic coast of this country, nourished by the communications which run down it. This particular volume is divided into three sections, the first of which deals with Gauley Bridge, West Virginia, where that dust disease, silicosis, took the lives of many miners. The Gauley Bridge situation, you remember, was the subject of a congressional investigation a year or two ago.

Sillen: Thank you, Miss Rukeyser. That is very helpful indeed . . . It has been pointed out that yours is the first poem of its kind in which a town with its people and its industries and its common problems has been used as the subject of a poem. Didn't Edgar Lee Masters attempt the same kind of thing in his *Spoon River Anthology?*

Rukeyser: Well, not exactly. Masters took the town as seen through separate, unconnected personalities, and tried to build up a picture through those. What I have done is to use a contemporary statistical method. The large unit is reflected in the lives of the people, so that you get an engineer and his story in terms of his work on the dam. You get the story of the Jones family, for example, from the point of view of the mother who saw her husband and her three sons becoming ill of the silicosis which affected the 2,000 people who worked on the project . . . She was the first one, by the way, to bring the matter to court and to the attention of the country at large.

Sillen: How did the engineers fit into the picture? They were not natives of the place, were they?

Rukeyser: No. The engineers were a representative type of what I should call society in the abstract. They cared mainly about the mechanical beauty and efficiency of the thing they were building, and not about the human lives involved or any of the humanities.

Sillen: That type of reaction to the scene was strikingly different from that of a poet's, then, wasn't it?

Rukeyser: It was different from my own reaction, at least.

Sillen: Miss Rukeyser, I think the poem called "Gauley Bridge" gives a good picture of the town as one approaches it for the first time. Will you read it?

Rukeyser: [Reads poem]

Sillen: The first part of your book is dominated by the image of silicosis. Will you explain this disease, Miss Rukeyser?

Rukeyser: I have explained the disease in a poem which is in the form of a dialogue between the doctor and his examiner on the investigation committee. Will you read the part of the examiner, Dr. Sillen?

[Rukeyser and Sillen read "The Disease"]

Rukeyser: I might add that one of the poems in this group gives a picture of the liberal congressman Jerry O'Connell of Montana, whose father died from silicosis when O'Connell was 8 years old. It was O'Connell who introduced a bill against industrial silicosis in Congress, where he pointed out that silicosis has assumed the proportions of a war in this country, with one million potential victims, and 500,000 persons actually having the disease in the United States.

Sillen: Isn't this an unusual theme for poetry, Miss Rukeyser? Most people associate poetry with what they call the pleasant things in life. How would you justify the use of such a theme as you have selected?

Rukeyser: I feel that it is on material of this sort that poetry must now build itself, as well as on those personal responses which have always been the basis for poetry. The actual world, not some fantastic structure that has nothing to do with reality, must provide the material for modern poetry. . . . This is heroic American material. The town of Gauley Bridge stands as a pattern for all those places where people are linked even in the middle of their suffering, where people fight against an evil condition so that other people need not go through the same fight. . . . I have tried to dramatize the congressional investigations because the human testimony produced there was so powerful.

Sillen: Miss Rukeyser, would you call *U.S. 1* a narrative poem? It seems to have some elements of conventional narrative poetry, and yet there are technical devices which are relatively unfamiliar to the average reader of poetry. How would you describe your method?

Rukeyser: I am glad you raised that question, Mr. Sillen. I am sure that it is one which may confuse some readers. . . . I think that it would be misleading to describe my poem [*The Book of the Dead*] as narrative poetry in the ordinary sense. I have tried to write a series of poems which are linked together as the sequences of a movie are linked together . . . so that during the sequence the reader has built up for him the story and the picture.

Sillen: How would you describe the difference between the movie sequence and the narrative method of a novel, for example?

Rukeyser: Well, I should say that there are two ways of telling a story . . . the one that is used in the novel and the theater, which is the method of straight development and unfolding of the story . . . and the other that of the movies and some contemporary long poems: for example, Hart Crane's *The Bridge* and Horace Gregory's *Chorus for Survival.* In this second technique, relationships are made clear in the same way that a movie shot of a city being bombed will show you first a picture of the plane dropping its bomb . . . and then will cut away to the ground and the explosion itself. The movie public has adjusted itself to this sequence so that there isn't any strain or lack of belief in the tie-up between the two pictures. And in the same way, readers of contemporary poetry are finding that the adjustment of this kind of writing makes for vivid and active poetry.

Sillen: Would you like to read a poem which illustrates this device, Miss Rukeyser? It sounds extremely novel and interesting.

Rukeyser: In one sense, of course, the entire group of poems fits into this sequence pattern. To get the complete picture it is necessary to read the entire group. Perhaps the poem on Arthur Peyton illustrates the device as well as any other single poem. [Reads "Arthur Peyton"]

Sillen: I see that our time is getting short, and I am very anxious to hear about your experience in Barcelona, which formed the background of the two voyage poems in the third section of your book: "The Cruise" . . . and "Mediterranean." Won't you tell us something about that.

Rukeyser: It was all exciting and revealing. You have already mentioned the fact that I was sent to Barcelona by a London magazine in the summer of 1936 to cover the People's Olympics. I was on the last train that got into Spain from France. It was stopped about twelve miles outside of Barcelona. For three days we were detained, during the battle for Barcelona and the rebel retreat to the French frontier along our railroad tracks. The train was a typical tourist train, except for the athletes who were there for the Olympics. Some of the English berated the representative of Cook's Tours for not telling them in advance that there was going to be a war. Then there was the woman from Peapack, New Jersey, who had come to Spain to see a bullfight and who got scared the moment they came through the train to search for cameras. A professor from the University of Madrid acted as the go-between for the train and the town.

Sillen: There must have been plenty of human material in that situation [for] a novel. And that accounts for your poem—"Mediterranean"—which deals with the evacuation of an international group from a war situation to an outer world and an equivocal peace. And it is linked also to "The Cruise," which is a poem about a cruise ship whose captain is ordered not to stop at any port which is doubtful or dangerous . . . a command which literally meant that he was unable to stop anywhere. I think it would be appropriate to conclude our talk with a reading from "Mediterranean," which has already been widely reprinted . . .

Rukeyser: [Reads from "Mediterranean" for as long as time permits]

Sillen: Thank you, Miss Rukeyser. I am sure that I express the feeling of your listeners in hoping for the success of the book which you published just this week, and which you were good enough to comment on in this program. Good luck!

Works Cited

Abrams, M. H. *The Mirror and the Lamp: Romantic Theory and the Critical Tradition.* New York: Oxford University Press, 1953.

Adler, Felix. *An Ethical Philosophy of Life, Presented in Its Main Outlines.* New York: Appleton, 1920.

Adorno, T. W. *Aesthetic Theory.* Ed. Gretel Adorno, Rolf Tiedemann, and Robert Hullot-Kentor; trans. Robert Hullot-Kentor. Minneapolis: University of Minnesota Press, 1997.

———. "Lyric Poetry and Society." Trans. Bruce Mayo. *Telos* 20 (1974): 52–71.

Allen, Philippa. "Gauley Bridge Death Toll Grows in Village of the Living Dead," *Daily Worker,* June 30, 1937, 5.

Allen, Philippa [Bernard Allen, pseud.]. "Two Thousand Dying on a Job." *New Masses,* January 15, 1935, 18–19; January 22, 1935, 19–21.

Anderson, Perry. *Lineages of the Absolutist State.* London: New Left Books, 1974.

Aristotle. *The Poetics of Aristotle.* Trans. Stephen Halliwell. Chapel Hill: University of North Carolina Press, 1987.

Aspiz, Harold. "Whitman's 'Poem of the Road.' " *Walt Whitman Quarterly Review* 12:3 (1995): 170–85.

Barnard, Rita. *The Great Depression and the Culture of Abundance: Kenneth Fearing, Nathanael West, and Mass Culture in the 1930s.* Cambridge: Cambridge University Press, 1995.

Benjamin, Walter. *The Arcades Project.* Ed. Rolf Tiedemann, trans. Howard Eiland and Kevin McLaughlin. Cambridge: Harvard University Press, Belknap Press, 1999.

———. "Theses on the Philosophy of History." In *Illuminations,* ed. Hannah Arendt, trans. Harry Zohn, 253–64. New York: Schocken Books, 1969.

Bernstein, Michael André. *The Tale of the Tribe: Ezra Pound and the Modern Verse Epic.* Princeton: Princeton University Press, 1980.

Bhaskar, Roy. *Dialectic: The Pulse of Freedom.* London: Verso, 1993.

———. *Philosophy and the Idea of Freedom.* Oxford: Basil Blackwell, 1991.

———. *The Possibility of Naturalism: A Philosophical Critique of the Contemporary Human Sciences.* Atlantic Highlands, N.J.: Humanities Press, 1979.

———. *A Realist Theory of Science.* Atlantic Highlands, N.J.: Humanities Press, 1978.

———. *Reclaiming Reality: A Critical Introduction to Comtemporary Philosophy.* London: Verso, 1989.

Bloch, Ernst. "Marxism and Poetry." In *The Utopian Function of Art and Literature,* ed. and trans. Jack Zipes and Frank Mecklenburg, 156–62. Cambridge: Massachusetts Institute of Technology Press, 1988.

———. *The Principle of Hope.* 3 vols. Trans. Neville Plaice, Stephen Plaice, and Paul Knight. Cambridge: Massachusetts Institute of Technology Press, 1986.

Bloom, James D. *Left Letters: The Culture Wars of Mike Gold and Joseph Freeman.* New York: Columbia University Press, 1992.

Bois, Guy. *The Crisis of Feudalism: Economy and Society in Eastern Normandy c. 1300–1550.* Cambridge: Cambridge University Press, 1984.

Breasted, James Henry. *The Dawn of Conscience.* New York: Charles Scribner's Sons, 1934.

Broué, Pierre, and Témime Emile. *The Revolution and the Civil War in Spain.* Trans. Tony White. Cambridge: Massachusetts Institute of Technology Press, 1970.

Buck-Morss, Susan. *The Dialectics of Seeing.* Cambridge: Massachusetts Institute of Technology Press, 1989.

Budge, E. A. Wallis, ed. and trans. *The Egyptian Book of the Dead.* 1913. Reprint, New York: University Books, 1960.

Callinicos, Alex. *Theories and Narratives: Reflections on the Philosophy of History.* Cambridge, England: Polity Press, 1995.

Casillo, Robert. *The Genealogy of Demons: Anti-Semitism, Fascism, and the Myths of Ezra Pound.* Evanston, Ill.: Northwestern University Press, 1988.

Cherniack, Martin. *The Hawk's Nest Incident: America's Worst Industrial Accident.* New Haven: Yale University Press, 1986.

Clark, Harry Hayden, and Normal Foerster, eds. *James Russell Lowell: Representative Selections.* New York: American Book Company, 1947.

Claudin, Fernando. *The Communist Movement: From Comintern to Cominform.* 2 vols. New York: Monthly Review Press, 1975.

Collier, Andrew. *Scientific Realism and Socialist Thought.* Hemel Hempstead, England: Harvester Wheatsheaf, 1989.

Conley, Phil. *West Virginia Yesterday and Today.* Charleston, W.Va.: West Virginia Review Press, 1931.

Cooney, Terry. *The Rise of the New York Intellectuals: Partisan Review and Its Circle.* Madison: University of Wisconsin Press, 1986.

Davidson, Michael. *Ghostlier Demarcations: Modern Poetry and the Material Word.* Berkeley: University of California Press, 1997.

Davis, Robert Gorham [Obed Brooks, pseud.]. "Archibald MacLeish." In *Proletarian Literature in the United States.* Ed. Granville Hicks et al., 325–29. New York: International Publishers, 1935.

Della Volpe, Galvano. *Critique of Taste.* Trans. Michael Caesar. London: New Left Books, 1978.

Denning, Michael. *The Cultural Front: The Laboring of American Culture in the Twentieth Century.* London: Verso, 1997.

Dos Passos, John. *U.S.A.* 1937. Reprint, New York: New American Library, 1969.

Eisenstein, Sergei M. *The Film Sense.* Trans. and ed. Jay Leyda. London: Faber & Faber, 1943.

———. "Through Theatre to Cinema." *Theatre Arts Monthly* 20 (1936): 735–47.

Eliot, T. S. *Collected Poems, 1909–1962.* New York: Harcourt, Brace, and World, 1963.

———. *The Three Voices of Poetry.* New York: Cambridge University Press, 1954.

———. "*Ulysses,* Order, and Myth." 1923. In *James Joyce: The Critical Heritage,* 2 vols., ed. Robert H. Deming, 1:268–71. London: Routledge & Kegan Paul, 1970.

———. *The Waste Land: A Facsimile and Transcript of the Original Drafts, Including the Annotations of Ezra Pound.* Ed. Valerie Eliot. New York: Harcourt Brace Jovanovich, 1971.

Filreis, Alan. *Modernism from Right to Left: Wallace Stevens, the Thirties, and Literary Radicalism.* Cambridge: Cambridge University Press, 1994.

Fishkin, Shelley Fisher. *From Fact to Fiction: Journalism and Imaginative Writing in America.* Baltimore: Johns Hopkins University Press, 1985.

Foley, Barbara. *Radical Representations: Politics and Form in U.S. Proletarian Fiction, 1929–1941.* Durham, N.C.: Duke University Press, 1993.

Fowler, Alastair. *Kinds of Literature: An Introduction to the Theory of Genres and Modes.* Cambridge: Harvard University Press, 1982.

Goelet, Ogden, ed. *The Egyptian Book of the Dead: The Book of Going Forth by Day.* Trans. Raymond Faulkner. San Francisco: Chronicle Books, 1994.

Gold, Michael. "Examples of Worker Correspondence." In *Proletarian Literature in the United States.* Ed. Granville Hicks, et al., 160. New York: International Publishers, 1935.

————. "Out of the Fascist Unconscious." *New Republic* 75 (July 26, 1933): 295–96.

————. "Wilder: Prophet of the Genteel Christ." *New Republic* 64 (October 22, 1930): 266–67.

Graham, Keith. *Karl Marx, Our Contemporary: Social Theory for a Post-Leninist World*. London: Harvester Wheatsheaf, 1992.

Gramsci, Antonio. *Selections from the Cultural Writings*. Ed. David Forgacs and Geoffrey Nowell-Smith, trans. William Boelhower. Cambridge: Harvard University Press, 1985.

————. *Selections from the Prison Notebooks*. Ed. and trans. Quintin Hoare and Geoffrey Nowell Smith. New York: International Publishers, 1971.

Häublein, Ernst. *The Stanza*. London: Methuen, 1978.

Hegel, G. W. F. *Aesthetics: Lectures on Fine Art*. 3 vols. Trans. T. M. Knox. Oxford: Clarendon Press, 1975.

Hemingway, Ernest. *A Farewell to Arms*. 1929. Reprint, New York: Charles Scribner's Sons, 1957.

Hicks, Granville. "Der Shöne Archibald." In *Granville Hicks in the New Masses*, ed. Jack Alan Robbins, 69–72. Port Washington, N.Y.: Kennikat, 1974. First published under the pseudonym Margaret Wright Mather in *New Masses* 10 (January 16, 1934): 26.

Hicks, Granville, et al., eds. *Proletarian Literature in the United States*. New York: International Publishers, 1935.

Hobsbawm. Eric. *The Age of Extremes*. New York: Pantheon, 1994.

Hudson, Wayne. *The Marxist Philosophy of Ernst Bloch*. New York: St. Martin's Press, 1982.

Jameson, Fredric. *Marxism and Form: Twentieth-Century Dialectical Theories of Literature*. Princeton: Princeton University Press, 1971.

Kadlec, David. "X-Ray Testimonials in Muriel Rukeyser." *Modernism/Modernity* 5.1 (1998): 23–47.

Kalaidjian, Walter. *American Culture between the Wars: Revisionary Modernism and Postmodern Critique*. New York: Columbia University Press, 1993.

Kant, Immanuel. *Critique of Judgment*. 2d ed. Trans. J. H. Bernard. London: Macmillan, 1931.

Kennedy, Ed. "Three Workers Films." *Film Front* 1.1 (1934): 10–11.

Kenner, Hugh. *The Pound Era*. Berkeley: University of California Press, 1971.

Kertesz, Louise. *The Poetic Vision of Muriel Rukeyser*. Baton Rouge: Louisiana State University Press, 1980.

Korson, George. *Minstrels of the Mine Patch*. Philadelphia: University of Pennsylvania Press, 1938.

————. *Songs and Ballads of the Anthracite Miner*. New York: F. H. Hitchcock, 1927.

Langbaum, Robert. *The Poetry of Experience: The Dramatic Monologue in Modern Literary Tradition.* New York: W. W. Norton, 1963.

Lentricchia, Frank. *Modernist Quartet.* Cambridge: Cambridge University Press, 1994.

Levy, Ze'ev. "Utopia and Reality in the Philosophy of Ernst Bloch." In *Not Yet: Reconsidering Ernst Bloch,* ed. Jamie Owen Daniel and Tom Moylan, 175–85. London: Verso, 1997.

Lindley, David. *Lyric.* London: Methuen, 1985.

Longenbach, James. *Modernist Poetics of History: Pound, Eliot, and the Sense of the Past.* Princeton: Princeton University Press, 1987.

Loone, Eero. *Soviet Marxism and Analytical Philosophies of History.* Trans. Brian Pearce. London: Verso, 1992.

Lukács, Georg. "The Ideology of Modernism." In *Marxist Literary Theory: A Reader,* ed. Terry Eagleton and Drew Milne, 141–62. Oxford: Blackwell, 1996.

Maas, Willard. "Lost between Wars." Review of *U.S. 1,* by Muriel Rukeyser. *Poetry* 52:2 (1938): 101–4.

MacLeish, Archibald. *Poems, 1924–1933.* Boston: Houghton Mifflin, 1933.

MacLennan, Gary. "From the Actual to the Real: Left Wing Documentary in Australia, 1946–96." Ph.D. diss., Queensland University of Technology, 2000.

Maltz, Albert. "Man on a Road." *New Masses* 8 (January 1935): 19–21.

Marcantonio, Vito. "Dusty Death." *New Republic* 86 (March 4, 1936): 105–6.

Mariani, Paul. *William Carlos Williams: A New World Naked.* New York: W. W. Norton, 1981.

Marx, Karl. "Contribution to the Critique of Hegel's *Philosophy of Right:* Introduction." In *The Marx-Engels Reader,* 2d ed., ed. Robert Tucker, 53–65. New York: W. W. Norton, 1978.

Marx, Karl, and Friedrich Engels. *Manifesto of the Communist Party.* In *The Marx-Engels Reader,* 2d ed., ed. Robert Tucker, 469–500. New York: W. W. Norton, 1978.

———. *The German Ideology.* Ed. S. Ryazanskaya. London: Lawrence & Wishart, 1965.

Matthiessen, F. O. "The Rukeyser Imbroglio Cont'd." *Partisan Review* 11:2 (spring 1944): 217.

Mitchell, W. J. T. *Iconology: Image, Text, Ideology.* Chicago: University of Chicago Press, 1986.

Monteath, Peter. "The Spanish Civil War and the Aesthetics of Reportage." In *Literature and War,* ed. David Bevan, 69–85. Amsterdam: Rodopi, 1989.

Moretti, Franco. "From *The Waste Land* to the Artificial Paradise." In *Signs Taken for Wonders: Essays in the Sociology of Literary Forms,* trans. Susan Fischer et al., 209–39. London: New Left Books, 1983.

Nelson, Cary. *Repression and Recovery: Modern American Poetry and the Politics of Cultural Memory, 1910–1945.* Madison: University of Wisconsin Press, 1989.

Newcomb, John Timberman. "Archibald MacLeish and the Poetics of Public Speech: A Critique of High Modernism." *Journal of the Midwest Modern Language Association* 23:1 (1990): 9–26.

North, E. Lee. *Redcoats, Redskins, and Red-eyed Monsters.* South Brunswick, N.J.: A. S. Barnes, 1979.

O'Connor, Harvey. *Mellon's Millions: The Biography of a Fortune; The Life and Times of Andrew W. Mellon.* New York: John Day, 1933.

Olsen, Tillie. "I Want You Women Up North to Know." In *Anthology of Modern American Poetry,* ed. Cary Nelson, 652–54. New York: Oxford University Press, 2000.

Patchen, Kenneth. "The Old Lean over the Tombstones." In *First Will and Testament,* by Kenneth Patchen, 61–69. New York: New Directions, 1939.

Peeler, David P. "Unlonesome Highways: The Quest for Fact and Fellowship in Depression America." *Journal of American Studies* 18.2 (1984): 185–206.

Pitts, Rebecca. "The Rukeyser Imbroglio." *Partisan Review* 11:1 (winter 1944): 25–27.

Pound, Ezra. *The Cantos of Ezra Pound.* New York: New Directions, 1948.

———. *Jefferson and/or Mussolini: L'idea Statale; Fascism as I Have Seen It.* New York: Horace Liveright; London: Stanley Nott, 1936.

———. *Literary Essays.* Ed. T. S. Eliot. London: Faber & Faber, 1954.

———. *Pound/Joyce: The Letters of Ezra Pound to James Joyce, with Pound's Essays on Joyce.* Ed. Forrest Read. London: Faber & Faber, 1967.

Quinn, Kerker. "A Modern Poetic Realist." Review of *U.S. 1,* by Muriel Rukeyser. *New York Herald-Tribune Books,* February 20, 1938, 12.

Rabinowitz, Paula. *They Must Be Represented: The Politics of Documentary.* London: Verso, 1994.

Radest, Howard. Introduction to *Felix Adler,* by Robert S. Guttchen. New York: Twayne, 1974.

Rahv, Philip. *The Myth and the Powerhouse: Essays on Literature and Ideas.* New York: Farrar, Straus & Giroux, 1965.

Redman, Tim. *Ezra Pound and Italian Fascism.* Cambridge: Cambridge University Press, 1991.

Reed, John. *Ten Days That Shook the World.* 1919. Reprint, New York: International Publishers, 1934.

Rice, Philip Blair. "The Osiris Way." Review of *U.S. 1,* by Muriel Rukeyser. *Nation,* March 19, 1938, 335–37.

Rosenthal, M. L. "Chief Poets of the American Depression: Contributions of

Kenneth Fearing, Horace Gregory, and Muriel Rukeyser to Contemporary American Poetry." Ph.D. diss., New York University, 1949.

———. "The Longer Poems of Muriel Rukeyser." *New Directions in Poetry and Prose* 14 (1953): 202–29.

Ruff, Allen. *"We Called Each Other Comrade": Charles H. Kerr & Company, Radical Publishers.* Champaign/Urbana: University of Illinois Press, 1998.

Rukeyser, Muriel. "Adventures of Children." *Coronet,* September 1939, 23–38.

———. "Barcelona, 1936." *Life and Letters Today* 15:5 (1936): 26–33.

———. *The Collected Poems of Muriel Rukeyser.* New York: McGraw-Hill, 1978.

———. "Death in Spain: Barcelona on the Barricades." *New Masses* 20 (September 1, 1936): 9–11.

———. *Gauley Bridge.* Typescript, Muriel Rukeyser Papers, Library of Congress.

———. Interview by Cornelia P. Draves and Mary Joyce Fortunato. In *The Craft of Poetry: Interviews from the* New York Quarterly, ed. William Packard, 153–86. New York: Doubleday, 1974.

———. Interview by Harry T. Moore et al. In *Talks with Authors,* ed. Charles Madden, 125–50. Carbondale: Southern Illinois University Press, 1968.

———. Interview by Samuel Sillen. Transcript, Muriel Rukeyser Papers, Berg Collection, New York Public Library.

———. *The Life of Poetry.* New York: Current Books, 1949.

———. Review of *Land of the Free,* by Archibald MacLeish. *New Masses* 27 (April 26, 1938): 26–28.

———. *U.S. 1.* New York: Covici, Friede, 1938.

———. *Waterlily Fire: Poems 1935–1962.* New York: Macmillan, 1962.

———. "We Came for Games." *Esquire* 82 (October 1974): 192–94, 368–70.

———. Weekly record for 1937. Manuscript, Muriel Rukeyser Papers, Library of Congress.

———. *Willard Gibbs.* Garden City, N.Y.: Doubleday, Doran, 1942.

———. "Words and Images." *New Republic,* August 2, 1943, 140–42.

———. "Worlds Alongside." *Coronet,* October 1939, 83–96.

Schaffer, Alan. *Vito Marcantonio, Radical in Congress.* Syracuse: University of Syracuse Press, 1966.

Scholnick, Robert J. " 'The Password Primeval': Whitman's Use of Science in *Song of Myself." Studies in the American Renaissance* (1986): 385–425.

Selby, John E. *The Revolution in Virginia, 1775–1783.* Williamsburg, Va.: Colonial Williamsburg Foundation, 1988.

Shulman, Robert. *The Power of Political Art: The 1930s Literary Left Reconsidered.* Chapel Hill: University of North Carolina Press, 1999.

Sinfield, Alan. *Dramatic Monologue.* London: Methuen, 1977.

Smith, Grover. *The Waste Land.* London: George Allen & Unwin, 1983.

———. *T. S. Eliot's Poetry and Plays: A Study in Sources and Meaning.* Chicago: University of Chicago Press, 1974.

Spender, Stephen. "Remembering Eliot." *Sewanee Review* 74 (1966): 58–84.

Staiger, Emil. *Basic Concepts of Poetics.* Ed. Marianne Burkhard and Luanne T. Frank, trans. Janette C. Hudson and Luanne T. Frank. University Park: Penn State University Press, 1991.

Staub, Michael E. *Voices of Persuasion: Politics of Representation in 1930s America.* Cambridge: Cambridge University Press, 1994.

Stock, Noel. *The Life of Ezra Pound.* New York: Pantheon Books, 1970.

Stott, William. *Documentary Expression and Thirties America.* London: Oxford University Press, 1973.

Terrell, Carroll F. *A Companion to* The Cantos *of Ezra Pound.* 1980. Reprint, Berkeley: University of California Press, 1993.

Therborn, Goran. *The Ideology of Power and the Power of Ideology.* London: Verso, 1980.

Thomas, Hugh. *The Spanish Civil War.* 3d ed. London: Hamish Hamilton, 1977.

Thomson, Philip. *The Poetry of Brecht: Seven Studies.* Chapel Hill: University of North Carolina Press, 1989.

Thurston, Michael. "Documentary Modernism as Popular Front Poetics: Muriel Rukeyser's *The Book of the Dead.*" *Modern Language Quarterly* 60:1 (1999): 59–83.

Trotsky, Leon. *History of the Russian Revolution.* 1932. Ed. F. W. Dupee, trans. Max Eastman. Reprint, Garden City, N.Y.: Doubleday Anchor Books, 1959.

U.S. House Subcommittee of the Committee on Labor. *Investigation Relating to Conditions of Workers Employed in the Construction and Maintenance of Public Utilities.* 74th Cong., 2d sess., 1936, H.J.Res. 449.

Untermeyer, Louis. "Seven Poets." *Yale Review* 27:3 (March 1938), 604–9.

Vogel, Jeffrey. "The Tragedy of History." *New Left Review* 220 (1996): 36–61.

Wald, Alan. *Exiles from a Future Time: The Forging of the Mid-Twentieth-Century Literary Left.* Chapel Hill: University of North Carolina Press, 2002.

———. *The New York Intellectuals.* Chapel Hill: University of North Carolina Press, 1987.

———. *The Revolutionary Imagination: The Poetry and Politics of John Wheelwright and Sherry Mangan.* Chapel Hill: University of North Carolina Press, 1983.

Walton, Eda Lou. "Muriel Rukeyser's Poems." Review of *U.S. 1*, by Muriel Rukeyser. *New York Times Book Review*, March 27, 1938, 19.

Wheelwright, John. "Muriel Rukeyser—U.S. 1." Manuscript. John Wheelwright Collection. John Hay Library, Brown University.

———. "U.S. 1." Review of *U.S. 1*, by Muriel Rukeyser. *Partisan Review* 4:4 (1938): 54–56.

Whitman, Walt. *Leaves of Grass: Comprehensive Reader's Edition*. Ed. Harold W. Blodgett and Sculley Bradley. New York: W. W. Norton, 1965.

Williams, Raymond. *Towards 2000*. London: Chatto & Windus, 1983.

Williams, William Carlos. Review of *U.S. 1*, by Muriel Rukeyser. *New Republic* 94 (1938): 141–42.

Winston, Brian. *Claiming the Real: The Griersonian Documentary and Its Legitimations*. London: BFI, 1995.

Wohlfarth, Irving. "On the Messianic Structure of Walter Benjamin's Last Reflections." *Glyph: Johns Hopkins Textual Studies* 3 (1978): 148–212.

Wolff, David. "Document and Poetry." Review of *U.S. 1*, by Muriel Rukeyser. *New Masses* 26 (February 22, 1938): 23–24.

Zabel, Morton Dauwin. "Two Years of Poetry: 1937–39." *Southern Review* 5 (1939–1940): 568–608.

Zipes, Jack. "Toward a Realization of Anticipatory Illumination." Introduction to *The Utopian Function of Art and Literature*, by Ernst Bloch, ed. and trans. Jack Zipes and Frank Mecklenburg. Cambridge: Massachusetts Institute of Technology, 1988.

Index